T0197316

Retirement

A New Adventure

Patricia Reid-Waugh

authorHOUSE®

AuthorHouse™
1663 Liberty Drive
Bloomington, IN 47403
www.authorhouse.com
Phone: 1 (800) 839-8640

Published by AuthorHouse 11/28/2016

ISBN: 978-1-5246-4697-4 (sc)
ISBN: 978-1-5246-4707-0 (e)

Library of Congress Control Number: 2016917831

Print information available on the last page.

I dedicate this book
in loving memory of my mother and father,
Maude and John Reid.

Acknowledgements

I am deeply grateful to Cherry-Ann Smart, Cindy Draughton and Dr. Lilieth Nelson who took the time to read the manuscript and offer invaluable advice based on their extensive knowledge and experience.

I acknowledge with thanks, the guidance given by Clare Levijoki on the formulation and articulation of the ideas, content and style.

I am also greatly indebted to Patrick Champagnie who made his vast technical expertise available to me during the process of design and production.

Special mention is made of Elmer Walker whose fascinating account of a family trip, inspired the paragraph captioned "Going Back to Your Roots" which is included in the chapter encouraging the retiree to "Tell Your Story".

To my relatives and friends, (too numerous to mention individually), who read the various drafts and gave many helpful suggestions along the way; I could not have completed this book without your sustained encouragement and unwavering support. I appreciate you all and thank you most sincerely.

Contents

Introduction

When I announced my plan to retire at the age of 63, my friends and coworkers were shocked. The word *retired* did not seem to belong in the same sentence with my name. I was known as energetic and vivacious, still in the prime of my productive years. No one could picture me sitting around the house all day in a drab, ill-fitting housedress doing nothing.

But I knew something they didn't. Growing up, I watched my mother retire early and then proceed to lead a fuller life, adding to her years of distinguished service as a teacher. She traveled; she entertained; she mentored; she was active in the community. Whenever I visited her she was always getting ready to attend some event, or just getting back from one. She was living life to its fullest and being her best self.

For my mother, retirement was the time to get busy pursuing diverse interests like those just mentioned which, in combination, sweetened her journey towards self-actualization. I decided right then that I wanted to be like her when I grew up. And so, having put in my time at the office, at 63, it was time to go be myself before it was too late.

We often do not realize how being in the workforce limits the ways in which we can be ourselves. Similar to caring for children, working day after day puts tremendous demands on time and energy. Our true thoughts, feelings, and desires become secondary to these important obligations. Even on vacation, a part of us remains on the job because it is difficult to completely disengage from the workplace, especially in cases where the office calls to refer or consult on matters within our area of responsibility. Oftentimes, the fear of returning to an arduous workload is enough to ruin a long-planned vacation. Retirement offers us the opportunity to disengage from all of that – and engage in what we love.

During the writing stage, I distributed this book to a few friends for feedback and one comment really stuck out - "This book is not for retired people. It is for people of all ages who want to learn how to live life to its fullest."

Indeed, although I have chosen to write this book for people in my age and stage of life who are faced with society's stereotypes about what it means to be retired, the good life really can begin at any age. I hope many younger people will pick up this book as well, both so they can begin enjoying life as soon as possible, but also so they can begin planning and have it as easy as possible to do what they love in retirement.

A note about planning: when writing this book, I intentionally chose not to cover the aspect of financial planning for retirement. Not because financial planning is unimportant. Rather, the earlier you start planning for retirement, the earlier you can make it happen. In writing this book for retirees, I am writing primarily for people who have already done their financial planning because planning for retirement needs to start much earlier than retirement itself.

For the pre-retired person who picks up this book, I urge you to investigate the many books, seminars and workshops available on the topic of financial planning for retirement. This book covers ways to see the world, make music, get creative, give back, get connected and lead the good life on any budget. But money does make things easier – and the more of it you have, the bigger your retirement plans can be.

I do not claim to be the authority on finding inner peace. I am no Dalai Lama possessed with the wisdom of the ages. What I do have is experience in creating a retirement for myself which allows for amazing travel experiences, acquiring new and exciting skills and fully participating in making the world a better place – all of which precipitated quite a few adventures along the way.

By watching my mother before me, I learned the importance of not taking my time on this earth for granted. Although I chose to write this book in the midst of my own retirement and direct it towards fellow retirees who might be wondering "what's next?" now that they are no longer working - it is true that all of the experiences chronicled in this book could be had by anyone of any age.

So do not wait to develop the mindset that your time is precious. Do not wait to look into the many opportunities within your grasp - even if you do not have a large budget. So many fulfillments in life come simply from being fully present - to ourselves, to our families, and to our communities.

In this book I will share tips, information and encouragement to help you live your dream - in retirement, or before it. I will discuss where you might find resources and support for some of the dreams you have - from making fulfilling travel experiences a reality; to becoming known for your skills at creating beautiful music, art, and food; to ways you've never thought of to make the world a better place through volunteering.

I will share resources that are new to the modern world; such as an overview of how technology can make travel easier and more affordable, and how the Internet can be used to learn, teach, meet like-minded people, and even help you make money doing what you love. I will also discuss the profound benefits to you and to your family that can come from telling your life story in any format you choose - and offer some tips about how to discover and share the unique stories you have to tell.

Many people - including those who are not yet retired - could fulfill dreams they didn't even know they had if they only knew where to look, or perhaps, if they had a little "push" from a friend. Let me be that friend. I can help you discover how to have fantastic travel experiences and find relevant resources to turn your dreams into reality.

I sincerely hope this book helps you become your truest self and is the impetus that allows you to get the most joy from life during your retirement years - and the years before retirement for those who are not quite at that stage in life.

See the World and Find Your Place In It

I started traveling at an early age. Those early opportunities put me in a good position for travel later in life; I already knew the joys of travel, and was not intimidated by it. To people just starting out, travel can seem like an immense undertaking, one that poses many questions. Can I really afford to be away from home that long? What if I miss my flight? What if I get lost? The more you travel, the less you worry about what *could* go wrong. In this digitally-connected information age, you will find endless resources around you if you get lost, miss a flight, or run into some other challenging situation.

After the first couple of wrong turns and flight delays, I found travel challenges did not bother me at all. Any challenging situation was just another hassle, like getting caught in traffic on my way to work, or having a meeting run over the scheduled time.

Oh, the education and knowledge I have gained from traveling!

I visited Nelson Mandela's prison cell in South Africa. Standing in a place where history profoundly changed for the better through one man's strength moved me to tears. I went rafting on one of the wildest rivers in Africa. I visited the "Church of Gold" in Italy; attended dinner parties in Sweden, and even learnt strategies to attending globally-coveted sports events at a reasonable price. Along the way I put together a bucket list of the many other travel opportunities I wanted to pursue. In retirement, with time and flexibility as my new best friends I am ticking destinations off that bucket list one trip at a time, and loving every moment of it.

In this chapter, I hope to share some of the practical tips and insights I learned in the course of my travels.

Always, Always Ask About Senior Discounts

You have earned your age - now enjoy it! I throw this out up front because age comes with its advantages. From airlines to hotels to event tickets, there is a good chance someone is offering a senior discount. So always look for, or ask, about the discount option before deciding what your best price is for a given resource.

Now that we have got that tip out of the way, let's start looking at the specifics of what you want and need.

Know Your Needs and Expectations

Different people can have radically different travel styles. I, for example, can live out of a carry-on bag for a month if I'm interested enough in my destination. I can sleep nearly anywhere, eat just about anything, and all of my health needs - though I do have some - are highly mobile and easily manageable.

On the other end of the spectrum, I have a friend whose back problems only permit her to sit in certain types of chairs and sleep on a particular type of mattress. She also has a sleep disorder that requires her to carry a large piece of equipment which needs to be plugged into an electrical outlet just to get her through the night. Clearly, the same travel accommodations might not be right for both of us.

Consider your travel needs before you get started. What amenities do you absolutely need to feel human? Do you have specific dietary needs? Can you sleep on a plane or train, or will that leave you exhausted? Knowing what accommodations you need and which you can do without is a good first step to getting the most out of your travel experience.

Choosing Your Destination

There are some fairly obvious differences in why people travel. Some are motivated by sporting events, others by theme parks or concerts or by the desire to visit relatives and friends. Still others simply want a taste of a particular culture. When considering what destinations are best for you, there are a few things to take into consideration:

- Why do you want to travel? Are you interested in a change - any new and interesting change, since every new location has new things to offer? Is there a particular type of event you want to look for? Is there a particular person you would like to spend time with, or a specific type of experience you would want to acquire?

- What is your budget? Do you want to spend it all on one major trip, or divide the designated resources so you can have many experiences?

- Which will be more valuable to you - quantity, or "quality" of travel? I put "quality" in quotation marks because the most expensive, in-demand destinations are not always the best. At times they have unique charms, but so do many places without big stars on the map. Some extremely popular destinations with tourists may even be too commodified and streamlined for the tastes of other travelers.

Knowing what you have in terms of budget, and knowing what sorts of destinations and experiences you are looking for will help you better plan your trip.

Shop Around

Whether you are looking for cruise packages, plane or event tickets or types of lodging, there is always more than one option to choose from when planning your travel experiences. Browsing the World Wide Web for something you are not used to looking for, like airfare or lodging, may seem time consuming. If you learn the tricks of the trade though, you can travel for lower prices, especially as a retiree who is no longer on a strict work or time schedule.

In this era of the Internet, it is possible to see photographs of your accommodations before choosing them. You can even look up restaurants, museums, and any other unique places or cultural attractions in a given area before deciding where to visit.

Create an Itinerary

By planning in advance exactly where you want to go, you can make the most efficient choices for transportation, lodging, tickets and other essentials based on your budget. You can also make the most efficient choices about the timing and length of your trip. Planning for longer trips will allow you to really experience more of your destination but a longer stay is dependent on your budget.

You may even find free resources online to help you do the work. For nearly every region of the world, at least one person or organization local to the area has figured out the most efficient way to see the wide range of sights they would want to see if they were tourists in their own country. Using online search resources can yield a plethora of valuable information for potential travelers.

Accommodations: Options That May Surprise You

Back in the day, there were two main types of lodgings: shady motels and expensive hotels. While expensive hotels still exist and probably offer the ritziest accommodations, the information age - and different cultures to which you might be traveling - have yielded new ways to stay that might be unfamiliar to you.

Airbnb is one fascinating business model which developed in recent years. Through this website, people all over the world who have spare rooms or properties can list them like hotel rooms. The results can sometimes be amazing, in terms of both quality and budget. For example, it is possible to rent a whole apartment or condominium for a price comparable to a hotel room. This is an option that even some business people use, traveling in groups and renting multi-room apartments to share the cost and get an amenities upgrade at the same time.

Airbnb bookings for longer stays are also more affordable since the cost for a month can be discounted as much as 50 percent. This way you can really experience the country and its culture for an extended period of time. More scenic and exotic locations are also available on Airbnb. I have seen ads to rent out little cottages on the rocky Maine seashore and ads to stay with a couple on their countryside farm all of which allow a traveler to enjoy picturesque surroundings and good companionship while gaining knowledge about the local area. All these options give today's traveler far more flexibility than in the past to travel on tight budgets or gain truly unique experiences.

In this era of Internet deal-making, the same rooms in traditional hotels and motels may be listed at different prices across the Internet. Internet-based services like Trivago, Orbitz, Expedia and Priceline (yes, these are all websites) now exist to search for special deals on hotels and compare prices so travelers can find the lowest rates on hotels in a given area. These Internet-based travel sites typically offer discounts if you buy airfare and a hotel room together. They even make special deals with hotel chains to offer their un-booked rooms at lower-than-usual rates. There is also the choice of booking the hotel for bed and breakfast only, enabling the traveler to seek out inexpensive options for all other meals.

Air Travel: Cut the Frills, Cut Demand, Cut Prices

As with hotels, we are accustomed to the idea that there is "one way to travel." We think of major airlines flying into major airports - which might be good if you have a 13-hour flight and want to make sure it is comfortable, or if you need to get from point A to point B as quickly as possible. These highly in-demand services are also among the more expensive options.

Understanding the role of supply and demand in travel is key to reducing the cost of travel. For example, did you know that tickets for the same airline going to the same airport may be substantially cheaper or more expensive depending on the time of day or the actual day you travel? Airlines also change the price depending on how long in advance of the travel date you purchase your ticket.

The demand for tickets has peaks and valleys based on timing – meaning, if you are willing to take a flight at an unpopular time of day or on an unpopular day when people do not usually travel, you might save hundreds even if you are comparing the price for the same airline and the same destination city. Most major airlines have a search option on their websites that list the best times and days to travel, and which airports are least expensive to fly into for the area in which you wish to travel. For that reason, when you are traveling on a budget, be sure to shop around for times and days that offer the lowest fare options.

Even flying into a city for a big event a few days before the crowd arrives might allow you to save so much on airfare that you can afford the extra few days of lodging and have more time to experience your destination for the same price as flying in when demand is at its peak. Location is also a strong influence on price, as dictated by supply and demand. Flying in or out of smaller, outlying airports might be substantially less expensive than flying out of popular cities. All the people who want to get in and out of the big city for business will be flying straight there, but you could save money and get to experience more of the local culture by flying into or out of a smaller town.

The ultimate expression of exploiting supply and demand to travel as much as possible can be found in searching for the "cheapest plane tickets to anywhere" - no local area is without its charm, and areas with a great deal to offer will sometimes offer very cheap tickets when they are trying to boost tourism. Airlines out of Iceland, for example, are known to offer $99 one-way flights from California to encourage tourism. How much is a journey to Iceland worth to you?

The one caution I would issue when searching for cheap tickets, is to check the credibility of third party (non-airline) sites before booking tickets. With the advent of the Internet, public commentary and warnings are usually posted online by persons who have negative experiences with bad merchants. These warnings should not be ignored, particularly if they indicate a pattern of poor customer service and a reluctance to offer full refunds for obvious errors on their part.

There is one other tip to finding the right airfare for you - and that is understanding the role of luxuries in air travel. Even though folks might complain about how much service and amenities have been downgraded on airlines in recent decades, many major airlines still have some "frills," such as in-service snacks, outlets to power and charge electronic devices, earphones to listen to in-flight entertainment, extra legroom or omnipresent flight attendants. These amenities contribute more than you realize to the cost of your ticket.

Budget airlines may not win any awards with big business people who are used to the lap of luxury, but they can be incredibly useful for getting from point A to point B quickly and efficiently. I have used the "no frills" Ryanair, for example, to visit Italy from Germany, flying out of the small outlying Frankfurt Hahn airport. This was a nominal airfare compared to what it would be had I flown out of the Frankfurt am Main international airport on a major airline. I also travel with my own earphones to avoid the fee to purchase or borrow from the airline.

Ground Transport: When Is It the Best Option?

There is a certain time vs. money trade-off between air travel and ground transportation. On one hand, if you are going less than a few hundred miles, there is almost always a ground travel option which is far less expensive than air travel.

On the other hand, such ground travel may take hours more than air travel.

On the *third* hand (yes, we have one of those now), more time on the ground means more time to see sights and have experiences. If you want to see more of what a country has to offer, not just its big-name destinations, road tripping it may give you quite the experience. Suffice it to say, for folks with the right mind-set, a longer commute is not necessarily an inferior one.

All the supply-and-demand factors that apply to air travel also apply to ground travel. As with airfares, bus, train, and cab fares may all be less expensive at less popular times. As with airfare, it may also be possible to substantially lower costs by cutting luxuries. Beyond the issues of supply and demand, just like in the area of lodging, our ever-changing world is also supplying increasing flexibility to help travelers meet their precise needs based on their personalities, destinations and budgets.

In many areas, buses are the most cost-effective means of ground transportation. When traveling within or between large cities on a shoestring budget, buses can't be beat – it is often possible to travel hundreds of miles for tens of dollars, or across the city for single digits. There are also bus services dedicated to sightseeing tours and tours to specific events and attractions. These offer a viable alternative for retirees who are either unwilling or unable to drive long distances.

There are areas, though, where buses may not be a safe option. Try to find reviews online of any bus service you are considering using and carefully read the comments of past customers in order to determine if the cost savings are worth it to you.

Trains allow you to take in the scenery, albeit from a moving carriage that you cannot get out of to walk around. They also often offer a faster, more luxurious ride than buses. By the same token, they are often a bit pricier - sometimes rivaling airfares over long distances. Over shorter distances, it may be possible to travel economically by rail when looking to move between cities that are just a few hundred miles apart.

Car rentals give you total control over your transportation. Cars allow you to go where you want, when you want. Car rentals are perhaps most practical where local destinations are many miles apart (making cab fares prohibitive) and if the destinations you choose to visit are at a distance from bus or train routes. But any area with open country that you wish to explore could be a prime candidate for car rental - getting a ground vehicle to use how you want, when you want, for as long as you want.

Of course, as a trade-off, finding parking for a rental car in a crowded city may actually be more stress than it is worth. In urban locations, it might be best to simply pay for a car by the mile and not have to worry about parking since in most destinations, standard taxicab services are readily available. There are also a number of hybrid transportation service models such as Uber and Lyft, which have evolved in the 21st century and offer certain advantages over the standard taxicab option.

These new transportation models allow anyone who has a car to drive passengers around their hometown for money. With drivers ready to go whenever and wherever you are, it is not even necessary to reserve a cab if you wish to be picked up and whisked away to somewhere else promptly. It is important to realize that currently, these transportation services can only be summoned using a smartphone – unfortunately, the software that allows drivers and passengers to find each other in real-time cannot function on a "dumb phone," as I affectionately call them. Whatever the model used, at all times, caution should be exercised when hiring private transportation services to ensure they are operating legally and subject to proper regulation.

Get A Smartphone

Smartphones can certainly take some getting used to. When I got my first smartphone just a few years ago, I had trouble understanding the concept of the touchscreen. I would press my face against the phone where the keyboard should be and actually hang up on the person to whom I was talking.

After having had a smartphone for several years, I cannot tell you how much easier traveling is for me. Smartphones can function as Global Positioning System (GPS) devices which give you on-the-spot directions for how to walk, drive, or take public transit from virtually any starting point to any destination. They are home to "apps" put out by many transit services such as airlines and bus and train lines which can give you travel updates and even allow you to book flights and rides, on-the-spot in real-time.

Smartphones can be used for Google searches, too, which can show you anything from what restaurants, museums, coffee shops, or hotels are very near to you, to what their phone numbers are if you wish to call ahead and ask a question. Apps for virtually everything are available on smartphones - even for translation, which can allow your phone to serve as an emergency translator for most common languages - even if its grammar is a little "wonky."

I will discuss more ways that a smartphone can enrich your life in my Internet chapter, "Get Connected." But one benefit I will tell you right now is this: if you know you experience a lot of anxiety as a result of being in unfamiliar surroundings, smartphones make it nearly as easy to navigate a completely foreign city as it is to navigate your hometown, and in most countries there is sufficient free Wi-Fi internet access to make this a cost-effective proposition.

Visit Friends and Family

Friends and family who don't often get to see you would very likely be happy to have you visit. They would likely be insulted if you opt for paid accommodations instead of choosing to stay with them. To be a gracious guest, it is advisable to pick up the tab for some expenses such as meal tickets, groceries, or special events. By buying your hosts tickets to a special event near their home, they might see something they otherwise would not have while enjoying a mini-vacation right in their own backyards.

Indeed, I find that hosting folks from out-of-town often gives me a new appreciation for the place I live – hosting out-of-towners takes me out of my daily routine and rewards me with new experiences without the need to go very far. So, whenever possible, stay with friends and family, but keep the tourist mind-set and look for exciting experiences the area has to offer.

Make New Friends

One of the most fun parts of traveling is meeting new people who are also looking to have fun. There are ample opportunities to do this. Whether you are staying in a hotel full of fellow travelers who are also looking to meet new people, or being hosted through Airbnb by some locals interested in being good hosts, do not be afraid to reach out.

During my trip to Venice, Italy, I made some unexpected new friends - two women who turned out, like me, to be from the Caribbean. We had travelled on the same flight from Germany and by chance headed for the same bus terminal. I greeted them out of politeness and immediately recognized their Trinidadian accent when they responded. They, in turn, recognized the cadence of my Jamaican accent. We struck up a conversation and discovered we were headed to the same hotel on the same mission, a two-day sightseeing tour of Venice.

We boarded the bus and talked further on the ride to the hotel. That was when they disclosed they actually resided in the Stone Mountain – Lithonia area of Georgia, USA, the very area in which members of my family lived. Meeting each other and swapping life stories, mine of the many trips to Trinidad and Tobago and Stone Mountain, Georgia, became an experience in and of itself. They were delighted to hear that my trip to Germany was to attend the World Cup Football Finals in support of Trinidad and Tobago, the only Caribbean team to have made it to that stage.

In Venice, we did our sightseeing together, enjoyed a fascinating gondola boat tour along the Grand Canal and shared costs where possible. Just as travel invigorates you to see new places as an opportunity for new experiences - it makes meeting people into a new experience, too. There are benefits to traveling alone and keeping your own schedule – but there is great value in reaching out to others. Making new friends is one of the most fulfilling parts of the travel experience.

Ask the Locals

Local newspapers and Internet websites can be treasure troves of information about events happening during your stay that are at, or near, your travel destination. One of the first things I do upon arrival at a new destination is to ask a local contact what's happening in town. Once, while visiting Guatemala on business, I found out a classical concert was scheduled at the National Palace during my stay. By finding this out from locals ahead of time, I was able to secure a ticket to attend. On a business trip to Panama, I was able to attend a World Cup Qualifying football match between Jamaica and Panama. Once you get into a new city or country, be sure to ask local contacts what activities and events are scheduled. You might be pleasantly surprised.

Learn Visa Laws

While the concept of visas may seem straightforward in that you need a visa to travel in a country as a visitor, agreements between various governments can make this less complicated. Through reciprocity agreements, some countries allow you to travel in their country, too, even though the visa was originated for another country. Or, under certain visa waiver arrangements, residents of one country do not need a visa to visit certain other countries.

For example, the single Schengen visa covers most - but not all - countries in Europe. Quite a few countries also have deals whereby folks who hold a U.S. visa may not need separate visas to visit those countries. So determine what countries you want to visit - and then determine what visas you will need to be able to do so.

Now that we have discussed some tips that can help you get around regardless of where you are planning to visit, let us take a look at some features of three popular travel regions.

North America – Active and Energetic

North America, in many ways, has the *youngest* energy of any continent I have visited. When you think of visiting North America, you think of the flashing lights and colors of New York and Hollywood hot spots. You might not immediately think of Canada's rich culture and the breath-taking Rocky Mountain Parks, or of the continent's natural beauty and charming smaller towns – but these can also be truly remarkable, and are not to be missed if you are considering a world tour.

North America has amazing natural wonders. Consider Niagara Falls - one can only imagine the awe felt by the first European explorers to encounter this thunderous scene. The Grand Canyon - words and even photographs utterly fail to convey the scale of this spectacle, with its vivid red, orange, and even purple sediments laid bare by the waters of millennia past. Yellowstone - the untouched forests not quite like any other on Earth, populated by bears, wolves, and buffalo.

One of the fun features of the North American continent is its world famous amusement theme parks. From Walt Disney World in Florida to Disneyland in California, and from Six Flags in Georgia to Kings Dominion in Virginia, these attractions offer exciting family entertainment that is especially suitable for multi-generational family fun.

Probably everyone has seen New York City on TV - the Big Apple itself, a tourist's paradise with an abundance of famous places. There is Times Square, bordered on all sides by colored lights and billboards like some futuristic movie setting or work of art. There is Ground Zero - the memorial to the terror attack that awoke the world to the reality of al-Qaeda. The MetLife and Yankee stadiums and the USTA Billie Jean King National Tennis Center, home to the popular U.S. Open Tennis Grand Slam offer exciting sports events. There is the Metropolitan Opera House for classical entertainment, Broadway for the finest in theatre arts, and New York City hosts several American talk shows filmed before live audiences.

I was recently in New York, and on impulse, sent a request to *The Wendy Williams Show* to attend the following day's taping, explaining that I was a visitor to the country and there for a limited time. I was elated at receiving the invitation within a couple of hours. The following day I experienced the excitement of this live talk show in person, and I walked away with several gifts that were given to people in the audience.

The list of North American wonders and experiences go on. Other continents have just as many wonders and experiences of their own, of course, that are well worth exploring. But just as it is for Americans traveling in Europe, there are some things it is good to be aware of as a non-American traveling to the North America continent.

The first, is that Canada and the United States are two separate countries having separate visa entry requirements. The second, is that the U.S. may be one country, but many of its 50 states are as large as your average European nation. So before you decide to drive yourself somewhere, you really need to know what you're getting into. For instance, it is a big deal to rent a car and drive from New York to Los Angeles since it is 2,792 miles from one city to the other one.

When considering a trip to North America, consider what sort of transportation you will need for each leg of your journey. Will you be staying within one large city? If you plan on visiting more than one, can you take a train, or are the cities far enough apart that you will need to fly? If you are visiting a smaller town or nature area, will you need to rent a car?

One other important tip for non-Americans traveling in America is this: understand the system of tipping. A standard, acceptable tip is 15-20 percent of your bill for a meal or other service. For really good service, more than 20 percent is a nice gift to especially excellent servers. There is one other tip for traveling in America that tourists there will welcome. While some countries, such as Japan, have complex unspoken social protocols and systems of etiquette, North Americans tend to have more of an anything-goes mind-set. Their advice to visiting travelers? "Whatever you do, it's probably fine with us."

Europe – Steeped in History and Culture

The cities of Europe just *breathe* history. The architecture is ornate, opulent, and grandiose - often reflecting ancient power and wealth. The cities of Europe have been in place and established for a long, long time. They had time to focus on the details; to build huge cathedrals and concert halls as a sign of their past civilizations' greatness. And even outside of the cities, you get a sense of time. Cottages dotting the European countryside seem to have inspired the very ideal that we see in old paintings and on greeting cards.

One of the most fascinating aspects of European culture is the monarchical system that exists in some countries, notably in the United Kingdom. A tour around the sprawling Buckingham Palace is a must for me each time I visit London. I still hold on to the hope of seeing a member of the royal family at close range to deliver my well-rehearsed curtsy.

One thing that is essential when traveling in Europe is to understand visa laws. Unlike North America, where you can drive for thousands of miles and still be in the same country, in Europe, it is possible to cross international borders very quickly. On one hand, this is wonderful. It is easier to travel from Paris, France to Berlin, Germany than from New York to Los Angeles. On the other hand, it involves certain administrative considerations that are more complex.

For this reason, the Schengen visa is a lifesaver. This visa covers the majority of countries in Europe, with the United Kingdom being one of the exceptions. The Schengen visa allowed me to visit France, Switzerland, Germany, Luxembourg, and Belgium all in one trip, for example. I found it fascinating that the city of Basel sits on the tripoint border of Switzerland, Germany and France. And so, armed with this visa, I drove from Paris to Basel to experience this curious phenomenon. I drove around Basel for only a few hours, but, had my passport stamped by immigration in three different countries.

There is also Rail Europe - a modern, efficient, high-speed rail system which is even faster than air travel for getting from one point to another. It is possible to have breakfast on the Avenue des Champs-Élysées, Paris, attend mid-day mass at the Notre Dame Cathedral in Luxembourg, and have dinner in a restaurant around Brussels' Grand Place, all in one day.

Culturally, it is difficult to talk about Europe as a single entity, because Europe consists of countless distinct cultures. It is advisable to read up on the culture and etiquette of whatever country you are visiting *before* you get there. Visitors be warned - Europeans are more steeped in tradition, and may not have the same "anything goes" attitude in regards to social protocols.

On a trip to Sweden, for example, I attended a private dinner party and had my meal brought to me because I had injured my leg. I was mystified when the server brought me just a tiny amount of food. I was even more mystified when he came shortly thereafter and asked if I wanted seconds - then returned with a heaping plate.

Later, I learned it is an important piece of etiquette in Sweden to take only a small amount of food on the first round until everyone is served, then, it is appropriate to go back and take whatever you want. Perhaps it is lucky for me that I had to rely on someone else to serve me. I could have embarrassed myself quite thoroughly if I had been left to my own devices.

The Caribbean – Fun-Filled, Rhythmic and Laid-Back

The Caribbean is unlike any other place. The fusion of African, Spanish, French, Dutch and other cultures, set to stew in a tropical climate for centuries, produces a completely unique experience.

Jamaica has given the world iconic personalities such as Bob Marley. Its natural beauty is incredible - the sea, the sun, the ocean life, the world-famous Dunn's River Falls & Park. The warm, hospitable climate breeds a laid-back attitude that's all about enjoying life. The blend of African and European foods yields tasty wonders such as traditional Jamaican jerk. The fusion of the cultures mixed with a joyful atmosphere yields wonderfully unique reggae music, making Jamaica home to exciting music festivals.

Barbados, St. Lucia, St. Kitts and Nevis, as well as other islands also have rich musical traditions celebrated through annual festivals. Trinidad and Tobago has a unique annual Carnival - a huge festival of color and celebration of life stemming from the combined Indian, European, and African traditions.

Many all-inclusive properties offer a wonderful deal on the Caribbean experience. They cover your hotel, food, and all the liquor you can drink for a single charge. But that is not all. There are hotel chains across the Caribbean that offer popular exchange programs where you can enjoy multiple properties at the same price you would pay for a single property booking. Retirement offers a wonderful opportunity for you to take full advantage of these promotions and explore the Caribbean. Cruise Lines also allow you to visit several Caribbean islands in one trip. The ships sail at night, dock on an island in the morning, and passengers have all day to explore the island before the ship leaves in the evening for the next one.

In Europe and North America, the road network is characterized by multi-lane highways and streets that are usually well-marked, well-lit and well-maintained. Public transportation is common and reliable. In the Caribbean, this is not so. The road network outside of urban areas is often narrow and winding, in some cases, extending through hilly terrain. With many of the islands being small and most residents being native to the island, the need to clearly mark streets for strangers is often not felt. There is also little demand for public transportation. Most things are close together, people drive their cars everywhere and no one is in a hurry. Private taxi services do operate, so learn your way around those.

If you drive or bike in the Caribbean, beware of the relaxed driving styles. This is also true of many places in Europe. Some countries are simply not as conscientious about road safety as others are, and that can be dangerous for visitors who expect other drivers to abide by the strict road codes and rules applicable in their home countries.

Travelers may also be surprised by the different languages spoken in the Caribbean. Historically, these islands were colonized by various European countries. The Caribbean people in several islands speak a variety of European-based languages with strong local dialects, but English is still the predominant language within the region.

People in the Caribbean are warm and friendly, always happy to see a new face that could mean a new adventure. The hustle and bustle of colder climes are left behind when you land in the Caribbean to experience the pulse, rhythm and warmth of its people.

Benefits and Risks in an Uncertain World

People are sometimes afraid to travel due to the perception that other places are more dangerous than their own home. The reality of course, is that frightening things are still very rare in most parts of the world even though they can happen anywhere, including where you are.

We can never predict where danger will strike. What we can do is decide what is most important to us. We could refrain from traveling within our own country, or overseas, because of the risk of crime, violence, disease or terrorism. But the real question is, what is your own ideal risk-reward ratio? How many slices of tasty pizza are worth the corresponding risk of heart disease? How many car trips out of the house are worth the corresponding risk of being in an automobile accident? How many trips out of state or overseas are worth the corresponding risk of experiencing violence while you're there?

Answers to these questions will be different for different people. Some people will undertake trips, even to areas that are known to be dangerous, because the experience might be worth the risks they are likely to encounter. A friend recently sought to interest me into taking a trip to include the transcontinental city of Istanbul, Turkey. I said an emphatic "no way" and tried to dissuade her from going, recalling the news of a terror attack occurring there in recent times.

She would have no part in my negativity, planned her trip with other friends and went. She has now returned armed with stunning photographs, videos and memorabilia from some of the world's most visited tourist attractions including the Grand Bazaar, Spice Bazaar, Blue Mosque and Dolmabahce Palace. I regret my decision not to go.

It is always wise to be informed of both the risks and rewards of what you are doing. No one should walk into a situation blind to the possibilities and realities. But ask: what risks are worth the rewards of travel to me? What is worth staying at home instead of traveling the world? And if, after you have asked those questions, you are reluctant to venture overseas, then become a tourist in your own country and enjoy it.

Unleash The Maestro in You

Many of us dream of making music when we are young, but ultimately abandon that dream for one reason or another. I had one classmate who desperately wanted to play the saxophone in elementary school but his family could not afford the instrument, and besides, I doubt his parents wanted to contend with the noise. Guess what his wife bought him for his 62nd birthday? A saxophone!

Picking up a new instrument or musical skill may not be the first thing that appeals to you as a great activity for retirement. It is the sort of activity that, at first glance, may seem too challenging to start at this stage of life.

After all, those of us who have put in many years in the workforce are probably used to being the expert in the room. Becoming a student again - picking up something new that we are not already good at – may seem like a recipe for frustration and failure. Because we are not necessarily guaranteed to be surrounded by other people our age who are also just learning, the prospect of embarking on such a musical journey may seem daunting. Apart from the joy to be derived from the music itself, a number of published studies suggest that the leisure activity of learning to play a musical instrument in adulthood can result in a reduced risk of cognitive impairment and dementia.

I was lucky enough to start making music at an early age. My parents enrolled me in piano lessons as a child and I loved the way playing music made me feel. As I got better at playing the piano I could tinkle the ivories and make magical sounds like a skilled musician, and my family and neighbors delighted in listening. It really did feel like magic. Music allows the listener to experience something that they otherwise would not - and being able to create such an experience is akin to being a skilled painter, writer, or architect.

As a teenager, I played the piano for my church and at school. Later on as a young adult, I learned to play the organ. I loved the technical challenge of this musical instrument with its multiple manuals and pedal keys played with the feet. But deep down, I had also always wanted to play the violin. The violin's sweet, expressive sounds kept calling to me over the years, but in my busy life there just wasn't time to learn the instrument. Now, in retirement, I have finally found the time to begin my journey with the violin. I am learning to create those sweet sounds I had yearned to make for so many years. The experience is thoroughly enjoyable for me, and I daresay for my teacher, as well.

There are many ways to make music - not all of them as complicated as learning to play the violin. There are simpler, easier to learn instruments that are fun to play including the keyboard, guitar, and many woodwinds. These instruments do not require learning whole new ways of using one's body, ways different from those encountered in daily activity. There are choirs and other singing groups which allow you to use your voice to create music.

To be able to communicate our feelings through music is liberating.

To set an atmosphere and change a mood through music is powerful. Mastering a new skill at this stage of life is refreshing and keeps us young at heart.

On that note, I want to address one of the common concerns for any retiree who begins a youthful venture like learning to play an instrument or joining a music group. If you are anything like me, you may be intimidated by the fact that most of the people you meet who are doing similar things seem like children to you. My own violin teacher has a class of mostly teenagers. I am definitely an unusual student in that class.

But far from having any sort of negative reaction, I have found the teenagers actually admire me for joining their class. Young people often react with warmth and admiration to those who are young at heart, who follow their passion and walk outside the mold of what people our age are supposed to do.

In this chapter, I will discuss a bit more about the resources available to those of you who wish to pick up an instrument or start to sing. I will also talk a bit about my own experiences with the challenges and rewards of making music in retirement.

What Music Moves You?

Different people seem to be drawn to different instruments. Perhaps it is an expression of our personalities. I was drawn to the sweet, sensuous tone of the violin. My former classmate was drawn to the rich, edgy strains of the saxophone. Others may love the intricacies of the piano, vividly recalling their childhood efforts to play "Mary Had a Little Lamb" or "Chopsticks." Yet others may love the gritty, pounding rhythm of the bass guitar that you can feel deep down in your bones.

So what would you play, if you could play anything? Is it orchestral music that delights you? Or perhaps the camaraderie of the big band, or the pulsating rhythm of a steel pan ensemble? Is it rock music or jazz improvisations? What songs would you sing if you decided to exploit your vocal ability? Do you have a passion for solo or choral singing? Are you moved by the elegant perfection of good a cappella singing? There is some music in all of us, and what better time to tap into our inner being, find our passion and unleash the maestro in us than in the days of retirement when we are in the stage of self-actualization.

Choosing Your Instrument

The number of instruments in the world boggles the mind. From voice to string to percussion, there is a way for everyone to make music. The question is, for which do you have a passion?

- Voice is, in some ways, the least complex instrument available to us. It is what we talk with every day. That does not mean there is not a high level of skill and complexity that can be reached, as any opera singer will attest. But there are fewer brand-new motor skills involved in learning to sing than in learning to manipulate a musical instrument.

  Are you a regular bathroom singer? Why confine your vocal antics to the shower? With a little training, you could experience the joy of pleasing family, friends and other audiences as a soloist, or part of a vocal group. If you look around, you will see many opportunities to unleash your vocal talent to friendly audiences within your community, at your local church and other places of worship.

  Be inspired by the Susan Boyle story. At 48, she signed up as a contestant on the show *Britain's Got Talent*. Her modest appearance did not fit the typical profile of the young, glamorous, up-and-coming singer seeking exposure through a popular talent show. But when she opened her mouth she shocked the judges, audience, and viewers by unleashing an amazing vocal range, and nearly brought the feared judge, Simon Cowell, to tears. That performance set the stage for the launch of Miss Boyle's international career as a recording artist and performer.

As with voice, it could be argued that every instrument has a great deal of room for complexity and skill. But anyone can tap a key on a piano and sound a given note, for example, while producing a note on a violin is not nearly as simple. It involves learning to hold the bow and the instrument in a particular way, and keeping the bow on just one string before you can even get to the point of producing a single note. The good news is there are many families of instruments which include both relatively simple and relatively complex instruments.

- Stringed instruments – For more casual and modern genres of music the guitar, ukulele and banjo are good choices for the retiree. These instruments can give strong supporting accompaniment to rock, blues, folk and country jam sessions, sing-alongs and family gatherings. With a bit of instruction on some stringed instruments you can learn basic chords and rhythms in fairly short order and probably pick-up and entertain a gathering sooner than you think.

  For classical and some other elements of modern music the orchestral string family, including violin, viola, cello and double bass is the popular choice of instrument. Be mindful though that more intense instruction is needed to master the posture, motor skills and technical aspects of learning to play these instruments. However, if, like me, you had studied some form of music in your youth, you will find that knowledge useful and transferable in many respects, making it easier for you to learn the rudiments of playing a new instrument.

- Woodwind and reed instruments such as recorders, fifes, flutes, oboes, clarinets, piccolos; and yes, the saxophone.

  The starter woodwind instruments for many are the recorder and fife; instruments which require similar breath control to singing, combined with simple finger placements over the instrument's holes to produce different notes. These simple instruments are sometimes considered children's or starter instruments, but their full range of nuance and skill is often demonstrated by entertaining musicians giving truly stunning performances as part of community folk and string bands.

Cruise ship passengers to Caribbean destinations are often met by lively folk or string bands made up of musicians who are often primarily seniors. They demonstrate remarkable skill on these starter instruments, kicking up a musical storm for arriving visitors.

The style of music you want to play also makes a tremendous difference. The saxophone is ideal for jazz while the flute, clarinet and oboe would more likely be your choice if you are interested in classical music.

• The more popular keyboard instruments for seniors to learn are the piano, and to a lesser extent the accordion, which also relies on the pressing of keys to produce its different sounds.

Advances in technology in recent decades have made forms of the "piano" much more accessible to the average person. With the advent of the electronic keyboard, hobbyists can now purchase a light, mobile keyboard more cheaply, carry and store it more easily than a traditional upright piano.

The accordion is one of those instruments tailor-made for fun and entertainment. On the upside, it is a versatile instrument suitable for most music styles and good for improvisation and, of course, more portable than the piano or keyboard. On the downside, it requires good coordination in using the hands to play the actual notes, as well as expanding and contracting the bellows to produce the sound.

But think of how many times you have experienced an accordion player filling the street with music or playing for donations near where you were boarding a subway car (albeit not always tunefully). Most of these persons are self-taught. With some instruction you could turn a melodious tune on this instrument and earn your stripes as the preferred entertainer for family gatherings.

There is a different level of skill involved in playing a high-tempo classical sonata than in playing most rock, country, or worship songs. But the average senior who takes on the challenge of learning to play an instrument does this for fun and, with some instruction, can master the instrument at a level to make this possible.

- Percussion instruments - Drums are the most popular choice for percussion instruments but cymbals, rattles, the triangle and the tambourine are also instruments that present some appeal in a group setting.

  Percussion is the heartbeat or backbone of any musical group whether it is providing compelling rhythm to accompany singing, or setting the mood and tempo of a band, orchestra or ensemble.

- Brass instruments are a good choice for men who will be intrigued by the feature of having to purse the lips and position the tongue on the mouthpiece and puff the cheeks to get the blazing, powerful sound of brass. The range of brass instruments include the trumpet, trombone, cornet, tuba and horns.

  Many teachers of brass recommend potential players try different instruments to see which feels most comfortable to them. Smaller instruments are sometimes recommended for beginners, as these take less arm strength to hold up to your mouth for extended periods of time.

  Whether showcased through Afro-Caribbean music forms like the Ska, Reggae, Calypso and Soca, through military and marching band pageantry or through the jazzy swing of the big band, the sound of brass is bold and distinctive. So take up the challenge of learning to play a brass instrument, but be careful to practice quietly to avoid disturbing the neighbors.

One final consideration in choosing your instrument is the cost of it. Most musical instruments are sold in a wide price range. Generally, the better the instrument, the more expensive it is. But the retiree who decides to learn to play a musical instrument does not need one that is top of the line.

You will find budget-friendly starter instruments in each category. The violin I purchased is one such instrument and it has served me well up to this point. When I become proficient enough to start earning from my skill as a violinist, I will upgrade to a pricier instrument.

There is also the option of purchasing a used instrument at a substantially lower cost. Even though this is usually a risky alternative at times, good bargains can be secured. The bottom line is that proper checks should be done to ascertain the instrument's physical condition, functionality and sound quality. This may require the input of some knowledgeable person to assist you in making a decision on the purchase.

In some of the programs that are run through senior centers or by church groups, musical instruments are made available for use without charge. The main drawback here is that participants might not be allowed to take the instruments home to practice on their own time.

Which Kind of Music Lessons Are Right for You?

Once you have decided you want to take up an instrument or a musical craft, it is time to consider where to get instruction. For getting a firm and correct grounding in your musical technique, nothing compares to private lessons. Although these tend to be the priciest option, they give you intense, personalized instruction to ensure your technique is correct. This is important, especially if you are picking up one of the more complex instruments, where a seemingly inconsequential change in posture or fingering makes the difference between a beginner's level sound and a great one.

In my experience, private lessons have allowed me to progress much faster on the violin. At every lesson I am being given lots of tips and detailed feedback, so practicing by myself becomes a matter of constantly cementing what I am taught. When inquiring about lessons with a private teacher, always try to negotiate a senior discount. Alternatively, if you can afford to pay for several lessons upfront, try to negotiate for an early payment discount.

Group lessons, unlike private lessons, have an interesting dimension of fun to them – you get to work with people at the same level of musical skill as yourself. New friends can be made and fun can be had when commiserating about the frustrations of a particularly difficult technique, or the delight of mastering it.

Are there any music programs or community groups in your area looking for folks to play one instrument or another? It may also benefit a new retiree to check out the local senior center to see what music programs are offered. While the thought of these centers may conjure up notions associated with the traditional stereotype of retirement, you may be surprised to find them offering a variety of vibrant programs.

I know of senior centers that offer lessons in piano, guitar, dance and other activities such as oil painting, sculpture, pottery, theater arts and more – which we will speak about in our next chapter on hobbies. The advantage of these programs is they are either offered free of charge, or at a fraction of the going tuition rate and instruments are provided for participants' use.

On the island of Nevis, for example, the Government set up a program to teach seniors to play the steel pan, a percussion instrument native to Trinidad and Tobago and popular throughout the Caribbean. The island now boasts a steel pan orchestra composed entirely of seniors who perform on occasions for the public. Likewise, a friend of mine worked at a hospital in the U.S. that had a Life Sciences Orchestra – a volunteer orchestra composed entirely of people who were employees and retired employees of the hospital.

For the particularly ambitious or budget-strapped individual, the Internet offers numerous free instructional videos on how to learn to play your instrument of choice. Some instruments can even be learned this way entirely – a friend of mine learned to play the ukulele almost entirely through YouTube. However, doing so is not recommended for complex instruments which may have nuances that cannot be corrected without the aid of a real, live teacher. But for instruments which are technically simpler such as the guitar, keyboard, recorder, or drums, you may be able to pick up all the important techniques just from such free or very low-cost videos.

Many musicians with YouTube presences will post demonstrations or lessons to explain how they get the sound effects they do, or how they learned to play a particular piece. These lessons give you some enlightening new perspectives and can also be used to good effect as a supplement to private lessons. For example, I surprised my own violin teacher by learning the technique of vibrato from YouTube videos before he got around to teaching it to me. I simply added the technique to one of the songs I was playing in class one day. That kind of passion for going above and beyond classwork is the difference between the teenage student and the senior and is likely to delight any music teacher.

What About That Song in Your Heart?

Have you ever heard a song that seemed just right for your current situation? One that expressed so perfectly your own ideals and feelings that you thought the songwriter must be a kindred spirit? Or have you ever heard the tune of a song to which your own words came to mind as a substitute for the original words? Well, if you have had these experiences, why not try writing a song of your own?

The idea of song writing sounds intricate, as though you would need to be a musical master in order to do it. In fact, it can be quite simple. Writing a song to express an emotion or idea, or commemorate an event, does not require extensive formal training. It mostly requires the courage to create, experiment and improvise. During your retirement years, think of the many milestone events from your life that are worth celebrating and commemorating; your wedding anniversary, your spouse's birthday and any number of other significant life events. What better way to express your emotions and feelings than through an original song or the adaptation and tailoring of an existing song?

There are two basic components to writing a song for the human voice: the melody, and the lyrics. We all have hidden poetic skills we can unearth to write words that fit well into a rhythmic structure. Song writing is as simple as that.

Start out with a good brainstorm. Just as you would when designing any product, the first question to ask is: why do you want to write this song? Is there a person or event you would like to commemorate? Something you would like to say to someone dear to you? A general feeling in your life that you would like to express and share? Write down the ideas, feelings, and phrases relating to the subject. The end product does not have to be a finished poem or word-for-word lyrical sheet, but you will have a good idea of the words you want to convey.

Now it is time to tackle the melody. Often people think there is some complicated formula to doing this, or some alphabet of music they don't understand. While it is true there is musical theory that can help you craft complex harmonies and orchestral pieces, in reality, that is not what most amateur song writers do.

What do they do? They simply sing a tune to themselves as they create, improvise, arrange and rearrange. So the secret to concocting a new vocal melody that sings to you is simply this: play with your voice. Technology makes it easier than ever for us to preserve our vocal meanderings for playback and refinement. It will not take long to hit upon some combination and sequence of vocal sounds that you like. With your audio recorder handy, you can turn these into repeating phrases complete with verses and a chorus.

The songs you write need not be of Grammy Awards standard. Family, friends, neighbors and other associates appreciate a personalized song where emotions and feelings coming from the heart are expressed through an original piece or the adaptation of an existing song. I have taken an original song, for example, and introduced a rap segment that speaks specifically to the occasion being celebrated. The result? An entertaining, relevant and well-received version perfect for the occasion. It never hurts to play with other musicians' music as long as you are using it strictly for private non-commercial purposes.

Take up the challenge and get your creative juices flowing. Turn your emotions and feelings into celebratory songs of love, honor, praise and thanksgiving for your next family event and I guarantee you will be a hit.

Beginner's Mind

The great masters of martial arts speak of "beginner's mind" as being essential to physical and spiritual development. The heart of the beginner's mind is described in many cultures around the world from Eastern and Western mystics alike, who recommend simply waiting and being grateful, and cultivating a quiet mind receptive to the truth.

In addition to being recommended in the search for spiritual truth, this mindset of receptivity and having no expectations is recommended for learning. It is easy to see why. Persons who think they already know how to do something are less open to trying new things and harder to correct if their technique is less than ideal. They also tend to be much harder on themselves. Few things hamper progress like having an idea of where you should be and then getting discouraged and giving up when you are not there. After all, the learning process is just that - learning. It is a process of discovery; about us, about our instruments, about the challenges within ourselves and the deep rewards of accomplishing something difficult.

It certainly felt a bit awkward for me to pick up the violin at this stage. First, I had to simply learn to hold the bow properly - no easy task - and to keep it on the correct string, which is not easy when each string is only a fraction of an inch from the next. For many long hours of practice I felt like a child in elementary school, and not altogether in a good way. Anyone who has heard a novice practice on the violin knows how awful the squeaks and squawks can sound. Many times I wanted to put in earplugs, but I pressed on.

A few months into this musical journey, I posted my rendition of Beethoven's "Ode to Joy" on my Facebook page in an effort to test the waters. Despite the squeaks and squawks, the comments of my Facebook friends were very encouraging. They all congratulated me on my new skill and even thanked me for sharing the performance with them. Though they acknowledged that I was no concert violinist at that point in my journey, they said my video encouraged them to believe that new abilities were within reach, even for "old dogs" who had not gotten to learn all the tricks they wanted to in their youthful years.

Spurred on by these positive comments I practiced long and hard, eventually achieving my first goal of playing the classical gem, Pachelbel's "Canon in D" and a local favorite, Bob Marley's "Three Little Birds" at my 65th birthday party. What a feeling of accomplishment! Now, well into my seventh decade of life, I am on my way to becoming an accomplished violinist. Just because I missed out on this opportunity in my youth does not mean I have missed out on it for life.

I hope those of you who have an urge to play music, sing or write songs will not be discouraged, but rather be encouraged by my experience. It is never too late to unleash the maestro in you.

Get Creative - It is Not "Just a Hobby" Anymore

The word *hobby* conjures images of some art, some activity, some "thing" you are not totally serious about; an amateur activity you engage in rather than something you pursue as a professional. We are always encouraged to have hobbies, but it is understood at some social level that your hobby is not the primary thing you do, and you only do it when there is time to spare.

The distinction between hobbyist and professional can easily lose its meaning after retirement. Now that you are retired, you are no longer obligated to spend 40+ hours per week on the job. You are no longer required to fit into society's pre-defined niche of being the professional

"OR", "ER" or "IST", you know; like the doctOR, the lawyER or the machinIST. Now, you can live more freely and pursue whatever arts and skills make you happy, in any desired combination on a part-time or full-time basis. This is what it means to have hobbies in retirement.

The landscape of things you can do as a retiree is truly staggering. The world would have seen fascinating images of former United States President George Bush Sr. skydiving to celebrate his 80th, 85th and 90th birthdays. Nothing is off-limits, except perhaps space exploration. On my bucket list is learning to swim. Once I have conquered this I would love to take up scuba diving as my next retirement activity. For those of you without such a specific, burning passion, there are countless ways you can be creative close to home.

Many of the same truths apply to any other hobby as those that apply to music. Teachers can be found in your local community. Senior centers may offer activities and classes specifically for people of our age and stage in life. Local colleges may even have course offerings and enrichment programs in which any community member can enroll. Some of these courses may even be subsidized for seniors. The Internet also offers numerous free how-to-do resources, as people skilled in every conceivable activity under the sun are fond of posting videos showing off their skills and how others can accomplish the same competencies. There is also a preponderance of do-it-yourself (DIY) tips for those who are gifted at repairing stuff.

For those of us who are not so ambitious as to take up scuba diving or skydiving, in this chapter we will discuss some of the other rich opportunities ranging from at-home creativity to wild adventures, which await you in retirement.

Get Fit – Healthy Body, Healthy Mind

Fitness sounds like a chore. It is something we are always supposed to do, but who enjoys it? Maybe you! Even if gym classes are not your cup of tea, there are lots of ways to get moving that are both relaxing and fun-filled. The ability to get moving and feel comfortable in your own skin turns out to be crucial to maintaining good mental health and high energy levels, especially when one is not running up and down on the job anymore.

If you enjoy competition and hanging out with the guys or girls, competitive sports may be for you. As with learning music, we sometimes think of sports teams as being something that only students or professionals do; but in reality, most cities have masters' level sports activities for hobbyists just like you.

A neighbor of mine played competitive tennis well into his 80s – talk about impressive! In addition to giving him continuing friendships, social occasions and even some adoring fans, the sport helped him to stay spry and energetic so that he could continue getting out and about and playing catch with the grandkids right through his ninth decade of life.

Seniors worldwide who were sports stars in their heyday have the opportunity of showcasing their physical prowess through participation in the biennial National Senior Games, also known as the "Senior Olympics." The Games are organized in age divisions 50 – 54, 55 – 59 and so on and professional athletes are not eligible to participate in a particular sport until 20 years after the date they last competed as a professional in that sport. Retirees who have maintained good physical conditioning and skill in a particular sport should consider participating in qualifying competitions that are held at the local level. If you are not an athlete, consider participating in Bocce, Corn hole, Archery and other tournaments that are also part of the Senior Olympics. Or, if you do not want to participate in that capacity, you can still offer your services to these Games as a volunteer. It should be a fun experience.

There are a number of other disciplines being promoted to seniors which improve the health of the body while also cultivating inner peace. Everyone has heard of yoga these days; and I've seen some very enthusiastic senior yogis demonstrating a variety of intricate poses on television. Less widely appreciated is the Eastern art of tai chi, which incorporates the best elements of yoga and martial arts to help seniors stay younger, longer, while at the same time cultivating a sense of community and well-being. A fun fact about tai chi is that its original name roughly translates in Chinese as "ultimate fist" That's right – this art which is offered by many senior centers was originally the nuclear weapon of martial arts, capable of kicking karate's butt.

It takes years of study to learn tai chi as a fighting art because it is the mastery of many subtle postures and movements which makes it so powerful in the end. But for retirees who generally are not interested in starring in kung fu movies, usually only the basic postures are taught. These basic postures may not put you on the fast track to vanquishing evil with your fists, but they are proven by science to improve balance, muscle tone, and overall well-being, preventing falls and even potentially staving off arthritis and dementia in senior citizens.

Dancing offers retirees another avenue for maintaining a regular fitness routine. People across the world love to dance. For this reason, there is hardly a city where dance classes are not available for all age groups, and especially for seniors. In addition, several fitness experts have produced high, medium and low intensity aerobics dance routines on video and these are available commercially.

Other fitness activities for retirees that deserve special mention are swimming and water aerobics. People with severe joint problems can enjoy a fun workout by allowing muscles to work without suffering the shocks that can come from jumping around and hitting the ground repeatedly.

So for any senior who is new to retirement, I urge you to look into some method of getting and staying fit. You may not think of yourself as an athlete, but physical activity is the key to maintaining good health and high energy levels to make the most of your retirement years.

Get Wet – Diving and Fishing

I mentioned my own aspiration to become a scuba diver as part of my retirement activity. I hope that aspiration encourages you to get wet as well. The beauty of scuba diving is that it allows us humans to interact with the breathtaking marine environment without having to worry about coming up for air. We can see and touch parts of our global ecosystem that are normally off-limits to us. We can get up close and personal with sea lions, dolphins, stingrays, manatees and other fun creatures and in the process collect priceless photographs as they pose for us and play.

If you are a strong swimmer and a lover of the sea, and facilities are reasonably accessible, then exploring scuba diving as a hobby is well worth a try. It will open up a whole new dimension to your understanding, knowledge and appreciation for the world in which we live. If scuba diving is not your thing, you can still interact with underwater ecosystems in a different way; by fishing.

Some people get into fishing out of a love for tasty fish, or a love for competition. But many people, I find, do it for sheer love of the great outdoors. There are not many other hobbies which demand, or give you a reason to wake up before dawn, get out to the river or lake, and spend quiet, meditative hours alone or with friends and family in the serenity of nature.

Some enthusiasts practice fishing in combination with a cooking hobby, turning their prized catches into delicious, home-cooked meals. Others fish on a catch-and-release basis, a practice that is mandated at some established recreational fishing sites to preserve the stock of fish. Some go fishing right in their own backyards, in their hometown's rivers or ponds. Others use fishing as an opportunity to travel, taking long trips to rivers, lakes and seas with friends. Some fish purely for their own satisfaction and peace of mind. Others have a more competitive streak and enter local and international fishing competitions, which are always fierce tests of luck and skill.

Your fishing exploits are not likely to be the risky, dramatic real life events we see portrayed on reality TV's *Deadliest Catch*, unless, of course, that is what you seek. Your fishing experience is likely to be an intriguing game of cat and mouse played by baiter (you) and baited (the fish), earning you bragging rights for each successful catch and giving a warm sense of satisfaction. The calming sound of the water and the peaceful environment are also likely to be of great therapeutic value; and while you are at it, why not write journal entries after each trip? I am sure you will have great stories to tell from your fishing exploits.

Get Wild – Hiking, Camping, Ecotourism and Agritourism

There is a lot of glorious nature above the water, too. Hiking and camping are time-honored ways to have new and beautiful experiences. For the younger retiree who loves adventure these outdoor activities can be very appealing, particularly for family outings.

What can beat stargazing in a dark forest where the Milky Way is clearly visible, or sharing the experience of roasting marshmallows on a campfire with family and friends? Hiking and camping are great ways to connect with nature, and with each other. There is no bonding experience quite like working together to supply your own basic physical needs in less than ideal conditions.

People have gone hiking and camping in their own local or state parks for years; and as the world gets more interconnected, new opportunities to spend time with nature in international destinations are appearing. Ecotourism is a way to see natural beauty that is rare and exotic. Many agencies offer ecotourism travel opportunities. Tours are permitted through such environments as pristine South American rainforests, protected African savannahs, fragile desert biospheres, and threatened temperate forests. For the avid coffee lover, how appealing would it be for you to visit Jamaica and take a guided tour up to the mountains where the world famous Blue Mountain coffee is grown.

To be certified as ecotourism, an organization or program must demonstrate that it does not damage the natural environment in which it operates and that it actually raises money to help preserve it. By turning rare and threatened ecosystems into a source of profits, just by their continued existence, ecotourism is offering a sustainable future for beautiful threatened species and offering us the opportunity to see them in their natural habitat.

Through a number of organic farm networks, a love for the great outdoors can also be turned into yet another opportunity to travel – and help out a community in need at the same time. Organic farm networks connect volunteers with organic farmers and provide opportunities for cultural and educational exchange. Host farmers provide food and lodging to participants in exchange for a day's work on one of their farms – which are located in dozens of countries around the world. In addition, if you just want to stay and vacation on a farm without working, Agritourism offers the retiree a unique bed and breakfast travel experience.

Get Artistic – Visual Arts, at Home and Beyond

If you are not the adventurous type, let us try something a little bit closer to home. Visual arts are activities that retirees can engage in within their own homes or as part of a community grouping. Drawing, sketching, painting, photography, ceramics and sculpture; there are many forms of artistic expression that can be explored.

As with music, visual arts instruction can be found close to home – in studios and classes devoted to art hobbyists, in your local colleges, and at senior centers to name a few places that are likely to have such programs. Unlike music, because the outcome of art is judged solely on what you can see, it is much easier to pick up the basics using free or extremely low-cost how-to-do books and videos that can be found online or in bookstores. Visual arts also permit more room for experimentation than instrumental music. While the sonic properties of an instrument are complex and not to be tampered with, visual artists regularly mix different media such as paints, fabric, paper and wood to create interesting new artistic sensations. In the realm of visual arts, truly, the only limit is your imagination. My brother recently enrolled in art classes in Florida where he resides in retirement. He was a scientist all his working life and I had no idea that he possessed any artistic talent. But with a bit of instruction and lots of encouragement from his family and friends he is turning out to be quite an artist, and proudly gifting his paintings.

Ceramics, sculpture and other hands-on art forms are a bit trickier to get into, as they require more specialized methods and facilities. For example, ceramics usually need to be maintained using special methods when wet, and fired in a special oven when dry to avoid breaking. But with pottery studios and classes available in most cities and at a number of colleges, it is well worth the investment for a lover of ceramics and statuary art to pursue this hobby in retirement. Working with ceramics is no piece of cake. A broken statue or an awkwardly lopsided mug on your first attempt will most likely attest to that. But if you find that you love the skill and intricacy involved in working with clay, seeing things you made set in stone forever is deeply rewarding, and the pieces you create can be passed down in the family.

Community fairs and exhibitions at both the local and regional levels provide visual artists with the opportunity to showcase their work and speak with other artists and audiences who admire it. You may even have the opportunity to sell some of your pieces and earn some income from your talent and efforts. If you are a lover of the visual arts, consider making this your hobby in retirement. As with music, the learning curve may be steep at first, but the fruits are definitely rewarding.

Get Dirty – Gardening

Gardening can mean so many things. It can be a side hobby in a windowsill planter or a full-time job covering several acres. It can be a source of casual beauty, a display of prize-winning plants, or a supply of fresh produce for yourself and others.

The first type of garden that comes to mind is the home garden. These are generally kept either for beauty, or for food. People who garden for beauty may enjoy having fresh flowers inside and outside their homes whether as a casual hobby, or a project on which they spend many hours. People who garden for food may merely be supplementing their cooking with a few herbs or fresh veggies here and there, or they may be producing much of the food they eat, taking the concept of cooking from scratch to a whole new level.

In today's world you don't have to own a garden to participate in the activity of gardening. Perhaps you have no land or simply do not want to be the primary caretaker of a big plot of land. Community gardens, which are often run by nonprofit organizations or local schools, allow anyone to volunteer. The benefit to being part of a community garden is being able to spend time in the great outdoors and have the rewarding experience of watching the plants you tend grow to fruition without having to bear sole responsibility for the garden 24/7. Some community gardens allocate a share of the produce to each participant, which can add up to a substantial crop. In some communities, the produce is also shared with food banks and shelters for the homeless; so growing food can be an act of service to others.

There are also other unique opportunities to conduct residential gardening in public facilities. Villages within the United States like Glen Ellyn, Illinois for example, manage annual summer garden plot programs through their Park District Departments. A plot of land within the village designated for the program is divided into several small units and allocated to residents on a first come, first served basis, or through a lottery system. The program generally runs between May and October, and the already nominal fee is discounted for seniors. During these months, garden hobbyists have the opportunity to grow their own vegetables in the company of other enthusiasts, sharing tips and ideas and enjoying great camaraderie. Do not underestimate the capacity of these small plots to feed your family well into the winter. My brother reaped so much zucchini from his plot in Glen Ellyn that his wife was able to keep the family with a constant supply of warm zucchini bread through much of the cold winter.

If you prefer flowers to vegetables, there is also a whole world of gardening out there for you. From growing roses for your own pleasure to being part of an entire culture built around show plants such as orchids, it is possible to turn gardening into a deeply rewarding art form. Flower shows can become another opportunity to travel, where the passionate flower-lover will enjoy the opportunity to meet like-minded individuals and see new developments in the botanical world.

There are other gardening techniques retirees may find appropriate to their unique circumstances. Where space is limited, container gardening, the practice of growing plants in containers instead of in the ground, may be the solution. Health conscious retirees may be interested in companion gardening, which is the practice of planting certain flowers and vegetables in close proximity in order to provide essential nutrients to each other that produce healthier and better looking plants. A successful garden can go a long way in cutting food costs for the retiree, providing goods for barter and trade with neighbors and opening up opportunities for making new friends.

Get Delicious – Cooking and Baking

Cooking is a delicious skill to have in your retirement years. Who needs to buy expensive pre-made dishes when you can make your own from scratch? Who needs to spend money on processed, pre-made and sodium-filled food when you can prepare healthy alternatives?

In many cultures, food is considered not just a necessity of life or a tasty treat, but a whole social language. Meetings to arrange business, politics, and marriage are held over traditional dishes which seek to warm the heart, as well as the belly, and tantalize the emotions, as well as the taste buds. Family recipes are passed down from generation to generation, with everyone knowing that only this family can create that taste. Young people growing up in the family learn to make their parents' distinctive dishes. Others may develop unique and original recipes to express individual passions and identities.

There are specific holidays in different countries where a particular food item is a staple at that time of year. A friend of mine who was born and raised in the United States tells me her roots go back to Norway where Lutefisk and Lefse are food staples for Norwegians. So her Dad always made sure the Christmas dinner table included those foods along with stories steeped in the heritage of that country. Experimenting with recipes like these can be a great way to explore world cultures and history and connect with your roots.

In Jamaica, the "Christmas cake" has a special meaning. It means that your raisins, currants, prunes and cherries must be put to soak in wine and rum before summer ends to produce rich, spirit-filled cakes for the entire family when baked in December. The result is a sweet and warming concoction that truly encapsulates the spirit of Christmas in Jamaica - a sweet, warm, and spirited place.

In the United States, the Thanksgiving meal has a special meaning. It traces back to when the first Europeans came to North America and found their European crops would not grow in the unpredictable climate and soil of the New World. Food supplies were running out. But with the help of some Native American Indians, the Europeans were taught to grow indigenous crops such as corn and potatoes and to hunt game such as the huge fowl known as the turkey. The first Thanksgiving was held by new immigrants to the New World who truly had something to be grateful for, the fact that they were not going to starve.

Every culture has its distinctive food and cuisine. Now that you are retired, you have ample opportunity to experiment and establish your signature culinary fare to entertain family and friends on the many occasions that pop up throughout the year. You may even want to consider turning your culinary exploits into an income generating hobby by catering to small office meetings and casual gatherings. This could turn out to be a very satisfying and profitable venture.

Get Fashionable – Sewing and Knitting

Sewing and knitting are arguably the two most clichéd "old lady" activities. But in our increasingly modern culture, they are not just activities for old ladies anymore. There is a growing trend towards the use of exotic fibers and fabric to make bags and a variety of other accessories that make fashion statements.

The Internet is full of examples of the many things a skilled seamstress or seamster can make; from suits and dresses tailored to an individual's unique flair to impressive creations of hats, bags, scarves, ties, hair adornments, neck pieces and earrings that complete an outfit. Sewing is truly a cost-effective way to create striking designs that can be worn by yourself and others.

Our society spends a tremendous amount of money on clothes and readily discards them if they tear, don't fit, or are simply deemed unfashionable. These discards can serve as raw materials to create new and fashionable items that are uniquely you. What of the blankets, throws, rugs and woolen knit jumpers that we discard and replace when seasonal sales beckon? These can be utilized to craft chic cushion covers and decorative pillow covers that accentuate indoor and outdoor furnishings by applying creative styling. Another novel idea is gathering clothing discarded by your kids or grandkids and making a commemorative patchwork quilt to gift on one of their significant life events.

As with the other hobbies mentioned here, tutorials available online are making it easier than ever before to get us in a creative mindset and think outside the box. There are even tutorials online on making a dressmaker's dummy customized to your own body shape using nothing but an old t-shirt, duct tape, and discarded newspapers. So don't be afraid to take up these "old lady hobbies" – and be as frilly or as fierce as you want. This is a hobby that allows you to "turn your hand and make fashion."

Pay It Forward - Volunteer and Mentor

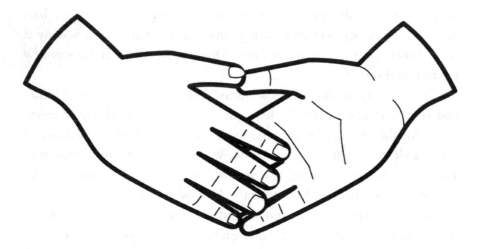

As retirees, we have a lot of experience under our belts. This is experience from which the world, especially young people, can benefit. Even beyond sharing our experience, the world can always benefit from people who have free time and a free set of hands to help make it a better place. In addition to making the world a better place for everyone, volunteering and mentoring has its own rich rewards for you. Volunteering is a great way to meet interesting and like-minded people, and mentoring is a great way to make younger friends and acquire surrogate children with whom you may establish satisfying and lasting relationships.

The ways to volunteer are almost limitless. Nearly every hospital, charity, school, library, service club and place of worship has room for volunteers. As such, the consideration is not how to find opportunities to volunteer, but rather, which opportunities fit you best.

Feed the Hungry

Food is a basic need of all people. Unfortunately, for some it is in short supply. Thousands of organizations exist to try to alleviate these needs; from Meals on Wheels programs that deliver food to the elderly and disabled, to food drives held by local places of worship and other community organizations, to soup kitchens and homeless shelters, to free food pantries operated by local and national governments.

All of these initiatives have some need for volunteer work in order to function at optimum levels. After all, one of the biggest costs of running any charity or humanitarian organization is the necessity to pay workers, so those of us who are retired and no longer need to work for pay can do the community and the hungry a great service by relieving some of that burden.

Another obvious way to donate your time to ending hunger is to participate in fundraising events planned specifically to support this cause. Many organizations each year hold walks, runs, and other fundraisers to create fun events, which bring communities together while also raising money and supplies to end hunger. Rather than donating food, some charities go the extra mile and donate farming supplies, instead, so that farmers in food-distressed regions can grow their own sustainable sources of food.

One organization fights hunger by inviting volunteers to package meals, which can then be shipped to food-distressed areas. They have found that a team of 40 to 50 volunteers working together in a fun, hands-on effort of teamwork for just two hours, can package over 10,000 meals. Assistance in sorting, packing, and preparing food is a common need in organizations fighting hunger. While individuals, churches and others may donate food, more processing is required to effectively deliver relief to hungry people in the local community or around the world.

Organizations such as the Red Cross and Salvation Army have a presence in almost every country. They have good track records in alleviating hunger at the local level. We see these organizations at work in our towns on a day-to-day basis and when natural and other disasters occur. A quick Internet search should be sufficient to help you find hunger relief programs that are currently looking for volunteers in your own hometown or around the world.

Protect Nature

Protecting the environment can be very therapeutic and great fun. Who does not love plants, animals, and the great outdoors? Even better, environmental protection is also a deeply humanitarian mission. The air we breathe and the water we drink must pass through nature to come to us; so if our natural environment is being destroyed, our own communities are at risk. Many people who live in poverty are already at risk from inhaling polluted air and drinking dirty water; and scientists believe all of us are beginning to feel the negative effects of climate change from air pollution, deforestation and other man-made environmental interventions.

Let us turn away from that picture to something cheerier – what you can do to help. Like fighting hunger, environmental protection programs can always use your helping hands. There are a variety of ways you can help from educating communities at home and around the world about how to protect the environment to participating in beach clean-up initiatives to helping clean up and build improvements at local parks. All of these efforts help conserve our planet for future generations.

Part of learning to protect nature, involves learning to understand nature and how people live in it. That is why some organizations offer volunteers opportunities to travel and have some truly unique experiences. For instance, you can help collect data for scientific research projects about exotic ecosystems or participate in archaeology digs to learn lessons from past societies. If you have a passion for science, volunteering to help protect the environment might be just the retirement activity for you, and one which produces tangible evidence of a job well done.

House the Homeless

Shelter is another basic human need, and one that is severely lacking in many communities. While hunger relief programs can attempt to feed people who are homeless or disabled, they often cannot house them or offer assistance in maintaining their own homes. To meet that need, our societies rely on local homeless shelters, corporate bodies and other organizations, and occasionally, very inventive and generous individuals.

There are a variety of ways in which you can help house the homeless. From helping raise money and educating volunteers and community members to actually building and repairing homes, there is no set of skills that cannot find a home in ending homelessness. The personal involvement of former United States President Jimmy Carter and his wife, Rosalynn, in building houses for the homeless through Habitat for Humanity International supports this point.

Habitat for Humanity International has been around for many decades and regularly sends teams of volunteers all over the world to help meet humanitarian housing needs. Volunteering to build homes and shelters is not something that needs to stay local. It can also become an opportunity for travel in association with a charitable or relief organization to help build or repair houses, especially in impoverished communities, or for those suffering in the wake of a natural disaster.

The major obstacle for organizations dedicated to housing the homeless is the necessity to pay staff. After all, a building pretty much just stays where it is; but many hours of labor are required to keep it secure and well maintained. Your local homeless shelters can nearly always use your help, whether it is by donating furniture, furnishings, utensils and other living amenities, or by doing maintenance work on the building and premises.

Your city or town may also have organizations dedicated to helping out elderly and disabled people who already have homes but are not able to maintain them. Places of worship and other community organizations often assist in activities such as painting and repairing private houses and even building wheelchair ramps for disabled people and the elderly. If you have a free set of hands, it is almost certain that there is someone in your community who needs some help.

Heal the Sick

Healthcare has always been one of the major challenges facing societies worldwide. Despite our best efforts, people continue to get sick and suffer from impaired quality of life, or even die from illnesses that are treatable and curable. You can probably guess what I am going to say – that the ways you can help to heal the sick are nearly limitless. You know that.

Healthcare is perhaps a unique area of volunteerism because it has two fronts which need assistance. On one hand, many areas of the world, and likely even people in your own backyard, still lack access to basic healthcare services. On the other hand, scientists are constantly developing new medical treatments, and they can benefit from your help in this regard, too.

The aspect of healthcare is one where raising money is a very important component of helping to alleviate the problem. Anyone can cook to feed the homeless or hammer a nail to help build a house, but it takes trained medical professionals and research scientists to give medical care; and medical supplies tend to cost more money than basic foodstuff.

As a result, one of the most helpful things you can do is participate in existing fundraising programs or initiate new and creative ways to raise money to improve healthcare. There are many venues which could greatly benefit from the money you raise, whether it is a cutting-edge research lab that can now afford more supplies to help them find new cures, or a charity organization which can now afford many more doses of vaccines to wipe out deadly diseases.

Another way volunteers can help reduce healthcare crises is by simply educating people about resources that are already available in their community. Many communities may have free clinics or assistance programs that the poor and dispossessed might not even know about. It is also a common practice of churches and service clubs, especially in underdeveloped and developing countries, to organize health fairs where medical and dental check-ups are offered to the public free of charge.

Retirees who are trained medical professionals have an opportunity to offer their services so that as many persons as possible can benefit from these free services. But there is also a role for those who are not trained in the medical field. You can offer your services to perform supporting administrative functions, which include handing out pamphlets and providing general counseling. Some communities and church-sponsored charities offer special training to help people become experts on healthcare resources available for the poor, and to help to counsel them. The offices that perform these tasks need volunteers to help with paperwork so that trained medical professionals can put more of their time towards delivering the actual healthcare.

One additional way of volunteering that may not occur to many people is to participate in clinical research. To learn more about how diseases work and to test new treatments, scientists need volunteers to participate in their research studies. These can include volunteers who do not have any health problems, or people with specific medical conditions that scientists want to learn to treat better.

Participating in such research to help improve public health can mean anything from answering survey questions to adopting a new health and wellness routine to trying a medication which may be brand new, or which scientists may be investigating for new uses in treating health conditions. Some clinical research may carry risks, such as those where subjects try out brand new, experimental drugs; but the majority of clinical research studies present minimal risk, meaning that you can help scientists learn by doing some normal, everyday activities while letting them monitor you.

And as you may have guessed, healthcare volunteering can also involve traveling. While one major need of international aid organizations and privately sponsored charities is money to buy supplies, they need helping hands on the ground, too. Retired health professionals who have a passion for healthcare are encouraged to share your expertise by joining a team that is traveling overseas to improve public health in a foreign country. By doing so you can travel the world and find your place in it.

Teach the World

As you consider volunteer roles in education, your mind might automatically focus on well-known philanthropists who contribute millions of dollars to build schools in foreign countries. Such grandiose acts of charity are unlikely to be within the financial means of the typical retiree. But what are schools, except places where teachers teach? And all of us can be teachers of important life skills.

An old saying goes, "Give a man a fish and you feed him for a day; teach a man to fish and you feed him for a lifetime." Of course, in our modern world, fishing is rarely the skill that is lacking. But, here are just a few of the many skills which can be taught to profoundly help people improve individual competencies, advance their education and careers, and provide for themselves:

- Teach basic reading to adults participating in literacy programs.

- Teach advanced writing to adults and teens to help them better advocate for themselves and obtain better jobs.

- Teach basic computer skills to adults to help them interface with the digital world around them.

- Teach advanced computer skills to teens and adults to help them get ahead in their careers.

- Teach English, Spanish, French or other native languages to help people interface with the world around them.

- Tutor children and teens in the more challenging academic subject areas such as math and science.

- Teach real life skills such as accounting and budgeting, to assist young up-and-coming entrepreneurs.

- Teach skilled trades such as carpentry, plumbing or electronics to assist young people in acquiring marketable skills.

These are just a few suggestions, and it is a good bet that most or all of those skills are needed in your own hometown. Many local communities have at least one volunteer tutoring program which is looking for people to help local children and adults realize their full potential. In recent years, public libraries have expanded their services by offering a wide range of education and enrichment activities and events for all age demographics. An Internet search on the website of your town's public library is likely to yield results showing programs such as literacy and language classes, résumé building and business classes, storytelling sessions, computer and social media classes, poetry reading and writing sessions, and so on. These are programs that present opportunities for retirees to volunteer their time and expertise as facilitators and resource persons. If you cannot find such a program, it may even be possible to become a freelance tutor. Inquire within your social circles or of educational administrators where particular needs exist and offer your skill to fill those needs.

Many foreign countries are on the lookout for people with English fluency who wish to help students learn "business English" so they can thrive in the global market. Japan, South Korea, and China, for example, all have highly developed English-teaching programs which import native English speakers to teach both children and adults. For the younger retiree, a stint such as this could turn out to be an exciting, enriching and lucrative adventure.

Pass on Your Wisdom

Mentoring is similar to education in that it is a teaching position, but it is very different from a class where the teacher is primarily concerned with students learning a single subject. Rather, a mentor is someone who advises younger persons on all aspects of their lives, helping them to grow and benefit from the experience of others so that they do not have to learn the hard way.

Traditional mentoring often happens in the context of a more experienced professional mentoring a younger one formally or informally. Perhaps there was an experienced professional in your field who helped you navigate career choices, work-life balance, and relationships in addition to whatever technical skills you learned from them.

Some organizations have formal mentoring programs which seek to connect older people to younger people in need of friendship and guidance. But the majority of mentorship happens informally, and occurs when a more experienced community member adopts one or more younger persons who they meet through a church, club, volunteer organization or other means. As a foreign student attending the University of Wisconsin, Madison, I was lucky enough to have met an older woman through a local church that reached out to foreign students, inviting them to sponsored events. Her help was invaluable in guiding me through this period of study; our friendship lasted until her passing many years later.

Of course, mentorship is not for everyone. But for those who feel they have learned many things they wish they had known decades ago, opportunities to share that wisdom with younger people are all around if you are active in your community.

Nurture the Human Spirit

People do not just need food, water, and shelter to thrive and live full lives. Indeed, ancient societies invented art, music and spirituality long before they invented healthcare or money. These very important components of life are often overlooked by people seeking to solve the world's problems – art, music, and dance are not seen as basic necessities of survival, so in the minds of some, why contribute your time to those aspects while so many other more pressing needs are not met?

The reality is, although we may not need the cultural arts to stay alive, we do need them to live a fully human experience. Art brings together communities, explores and celebrates emotions and identities, and uplifts the human spirit. So the proposal I am about to make is not frivolous. If you are able to volunteer to bring art to those who may not have many luxuries in their lives, this is a very valuable service.

Many homeless shelters or other programs for those who are disadvantaged are happy to have musical, visual, or performing arts brought to their constituents. If you are a performer – perhaps having unleashed your inner maestro – a simple musical performance could make people who so often lack access to necessities, let alone luxuries, feel truly special for an evening.

On the other hand, if you know of, or become involved with a local performing group such as an orchestra, theatre guild, or band, another wonderful way to enrich the lives of those in need is to offer a small number of free tickets to residents of local shelters or children's homes. By raising funds to purchase tickets or soliciting donations of tickets to performances in your local area, you can give people who would not ordinarily have the opportunity a chance to see live entertainment. It truly makes a difference in their lives as they go through their struggles.

My church, for example, invites a small group from a local homeless shelter to attend the annual Christmas play each year. I have also had success in soliciting donations of tickets from friends to enable people from the shelter to attend light local theatrical performances. Of course, critical to this initiative, is the need to arrange for transportation to and from the venue and the provision of refreshment during an intermission. But the unreserved joy displayed by the recipients far outweighs any costs incurred in providing this treat.

Remember, humanity is not just made of flesh and blood. We also need a sense of community, and a sense of being treated as something more than biological beings. Bringing art, music, and perhaps most importantly – consideration and recognition – to those who are accustomed to being overlooked, is an invaluable boost to the human spirit.

Get Connected - The Joy of the Internet

I have encountered a wide variety of attitudes towards the Internet among our league of seniors. Some find it an excellent tool for making the most of their daily lives, and are more digital creatures than their own children. Others remain suspicious of this new technology, or perhaps simply don't feel it is worth their time and effort to take it on at this stage, having lived without it all their lives. To this group, I say, "think again."

As with all things in life, getting the most out of the Internet is about balance. Stories abound of the negative results when teens use the Internet irresponsibly and without proper supervision. But stories also abound of touching examples of goodness made possible by the Internet. Meaningful connections can be fostered and lives enriched by relationships the modern digital world facilitates.

The Internet has truly ushered in the end of censorship and a new era of random acts of kindness. It enables people to display their work in a public space that has no borders. It changed the face of commerce by providing a worldwide marketplace for anything anyone has to offer for sale or give away for free. It has opened up a gateway to instant communication and provided a forum for information sharing. The Internet is all this and more.

But that is the big picture.

You may not be an aspiring hacker, or perhaps you only desire to spend a few minutes each day in front of a computer. In this chapter, I will endeavor to show you how to make the most of those few minutes - from seeing friends and family even when you cannot visit in person, to having access to worlds of information at your fingertips. I believe the World Wide Web has great potential to enrich the life of every retiree.

Say it with Email

Though there is a special touch to a handwritten letter that can't quite be replicated in print, snail mail, as we now call it, has one important drawback. That, of course, is time. Having to wait weeks while your letter is delivered, and then wait for a response to be sent back to you may be worth it sometimes. A friend of mine in the United States sent me a handwritten love letter asking me to post this from Jamaica to his wife's business address as a surprise. Now that is worth waiting for! But on a day-to-day basis, quick communication and rapid responses are definitely favored.

With email, writing a message to a friend or family member is as simple as typing on a keyboard. Just hit "send" and your message is delivered in seconds. The recipient can respond just as quickly, allowing the exchange of several "letters" in any one day, if you so desire.

Email also enables you to send things that arguably would not fit very well into an envelope – such as videos, sound bites, and attractive animations. With most computers and smartphones now equipped with sound-recording software, you can send a song, a spoken greeting, or a customized animation as easily as you can send text. At that point, you might wonder, "Why not just call?" Calling is nice too, but emailing an audio or video file makes it easier for the recipient to save the file forever and share it with others, if desired.

As technology has advanced, email has also found more ways to improve our lives. In addition to talking to people via electronic letters, many email providers now offer other important services. There is a calendar we can maintain which automatically sends us email reminders of upcoming events, and which we can even share electronically with other people interested in the event.

Of course, like postal mail, email has come to encompass more than personal communications. Many websites and organizations, online or offline, will ask for your email address when you engage with them. For some, this verifies that you are a real person and not a pre-set, computerized program surfing their website. For others, collecting email addresses allows them to send you updates about events and activities. And just like with your postal address, your email address may become the target of unwanted advertisements referred to as *spam*. Just think of those emails like the unwanted credit card offers you get periodically by post, and simply delete them.

In the early days of the Internet, it was recommended that persons never give so much as their real name out to people they met on the Internet. After all, you don't know for sure if those people are who they say they are. These days, security concerns have eased up a lot because people realize that interacting online is no riskier than interacting in person, but you still probably wouldn't give your home address to a random person you meet on the street. The same caution applies to people you communicate with by email.

That is why many people give a fake last name when signing up for an email address, or have a separate email address they give to strangers. In this way, you can keep in touch with someone you met online without having to give them information leading to your physical location. In spite of these cautions, email can assist us in improving the efficiency and effectiveness of our communication and enable us to keep in touch with those who mean the most to us.

Meet, Greet and Tweet!

Over the years, the primary seat of our "online identity" has shifted from email to what is termed as social media. Simply put, social media is the collection of online websites and networking applications (apps) that allow people to create, share and exchange information and establish social contacts. Once, email was the best (and sometimes only) way to keep in touch with someone using the power of the Internet. But now, the easiest way to contact people is often through social media sites where users create profiles of themselves.

Some of the more popular social media networking applications that exist today are Facebook, Twitter, Snapchat, Instagram, Facetime, WhatsApp, Google Hangouts and LinkedIn. With the rapid and ongoing changes in technology, new applications are constantly emerging that use the same basic concept of allowing users to see and share photographs and news, and instantly talk with friends and family. In a very real way this has become the new social sphere.

Importantly, social media opened the door to finding long-lost friends and relatives. If someone's social media profile is listed under their real name (most people's are), you might be able to search for, find and contact long-lost acquaintances, schoolmates, family friends and family. That is the most compelling reason for retirees to engage with social media. Many of us have lost touch with persons we cared for, not by choice, but simply because circumstances took us in different directions. Social media sites provide us with a chance to reconnect, and rekindle those friendships.

The British romantic drama TV series *Last Tango in Halifax* depicts this very exciting outcome. The storyline tells of widowed seniors in their seventies, once childhood sweethearts, who reunite through Facebook, and find passionate love again, even in the midst of the inevitable family drama. The story is actually based on the personal experience of the screenwriter's mother who lost touch with an old flame in their teenage years. Sixty years later, they reconnected through a social networking site, rekindled their love affair and married within six months, living "happily ever after." The power of social media to connect, reconnect and enrich lives should not be underestimated.

Social media has different privacy settings for those who are concerned about exposing all their information to the world. When setting up accounts on the various social media websites you can choose specific privacy settings that limit which photographs, pieces of information, and updates you post will be shared with the public and which will be visible only to those people whose friend requests you have chosen to accept. You can even make custom audiences for some material, allowing only family members and certain friends to see some of your content.

For me, social media has become a great way to stay connected and share aspects of my life with people who may not otherwise get to see it. You may recall in the chapter on music that I mentioned posting on Facebook the first audio clip of me playing the violin to get feedback from my friends. In this way dozens of people were able to hear my early playing (and if this sounds horrifying to you, remember - I only chose to share the clip because I was ready for an audience).

This story just scratches the surface of what makes social media so great, and so widely used. It is a wonderful way for relatives to keep on top of the academic achievements of family members, sports trophies won, engagements, graduations and a host of other life events. Social media gives us the opportunity to congratulate those lucky and hard-working people who have good news to share, and to offer condolences and support to those who may be going through hard times or bereavement.

Of course, social media is not all sunshine and roses. Mindful use is important. Some people engage in inflammatory arguments, particularly when articles and comments about subjects such as politics and religion are publicly posted and shared. But how you use social media is entirely up to you: it is easily possible to refrain from those discussions.

Some folks complain about oversharing on social media, citing annoyance with the constant stream of photographs, opinions, and updates on people's lives. But my mantra is that all things should be done in moderation. If you are becoming frustrated by how much you see of your friends and family on social media, perhaps *you* are spending too much time on it.

When I was growing up, tweeting was something that only birds did. Today, it has become the term for when people write short and to-the-point messages about a given subject, and "tweet" them to the Internet through the online community of Twitter. It distributes these "tweets" based on two parameters; the accounts of other users who you choose to "follow" and the hashtags you use to indicate topics of interest.

Hashtags are keywords or phrases, starting with the symbol "#" (which is how Twitter knows which words in a tweet are meant as hashtags). Using Twitter, people desiring to talk about any given subject with a larger community can tweet with that hashtag attached, and others with the same hashtag will see their tweets and be able to respond. Following the Twitter accounts of businesses, public service organizations, news sources and celebrities in whom you have an interest will yield a constant stream of information on what is happening worldwide and get you the inside scoop on most topics in real time.

So be it serious or silly; for connecting or reconnecting; to congratulate or console; meeting, greeting and tweeting through the Internet are social activities that retirees can find beneficial and enjoyable.

Be There, Even When You Can't

We are accustomed to telephones being the way to communicate across distances. Standard telephony was the go-to medium for long-distance communication before the Internet took its modern form. Once, computers could only be used to communicate with other people who had these expensive devices, and then only by using text. Now, information technology is so good that voices and even real-time video can be sent over the Internet for free or at nominal rates.

The benefits of using the Internet to communicate across time and space instead of using a standard phone plan, are many. Among other things, the infrastructure of the Internet actually makes using it the more affordable option. Whereas standard phone providers charge long-distance rates for calling across time zones and continents, the Internet sends massive amounts of data to anywhere in the world.

Thanks to these increases in data capabilities, chatting on our computer has come to take on a whole new meaning. Where once it meant simply typing words back and forth on a screen, now the ability to actually turn on a video camera and converse in real-time across miles is becoming more and more common.

Social networking services and video telephony applications such as

Skype, Facebook, Google Hangouts and many others, as well as devices such as laptops and smartphones, are now allowing people to speak face-to-face with increasing ease from any location as long as Internet access is available on the device. If you buy a new smartphone or laptop today, it is rare for it not to come with a webcam built-in which is the face-to-face feature.

This has allowed seniors to experience bold new innovations. You can have dinner with your children and grandchildren who live hundreds or even thousands of miles away by simply placing an open laptop or electronic tablet at the respective dinner tables with a video chat app running. They can see and hear you and you can see and hear them.

I have also seen the joy of video chatting used to ensure that people could be in attendance at important events, even if they had to be on another continent at the time. Can you imagine enjoying your grandchild's birthday party, even if it is happening hundreds of miles away and you are unable to be there in person? Can you imagine telling your grandchild a bedtime story from across the Atlantic or Pacific Ocean and watching that child drift off to sleep?

Of course, video chatting does not replace the benefits of personal contact. But attending an event via webcam is better than not being there at all, if making the trip is not an option.

Find Your Tribe

One much-celebrated benefit of the Internet is its ability to bring together like-minded people, even across continents. When looking for people who share your hobbies and passions, you are no longer restricted to who might live in your particular city. Many Internet venues serve as gathering places for people who are enthusiastic about virtually everything.

Online communities live right on the big social media sites which allows the set-up of any interest group. Some groups can look like debate forums, book clubs or social support groups. There is also a good chance your high school, college alumni association or military unit has set up a group on social media through which it connects with past students or members and promotes its activities. In fact, this is how the main characters in *Last Tango in Halifax* were depicted to reconnect; through Friends

Reunited, a website designed to reunite people who had in common a school, university, sports club, armed service or other grouping.

Groups tend to develop their own personality over time, depending on the personalities of the people who created them, and it can take a while to find a group that is right for you. But I have some very rewarding experiences meeting like-minded people from all over the world in such groups. For example, in preparation for writing this book, I joined a publishing group on Facebook to get some useful information and tips on the process. The encouragement and support of the group was priceless in this process. I also find discussions in forums devoted to diabetes management and my other health concerns particularly helpful.

Of course, it is important to exercise a reasonable degree of caution and be prepared to assert boundaries when meeting new people online. Though 99 percent of the people in online communities are real people just like yourself, you should initially interact with people you meet online just like you do with people you meet in a public place in real life. But while in real life it may be easy to tell if someone is a shady character, it is easier to hide character online, so exercise caution when giving out your personal information to people you meet on the Internet. If an interaction doesn't feel right, you are fully justified and smart to get out of there.

The World's Biggest Newsroom

The Internet makes it easier than ever before for people to find out what is going on in the world. Most major local and international news websites have developed their own apps, which will send breaking news updates in real-time to your email inbox or smartphone. You can even pick what kind of events you want to hear about.

The Internet also provides unique opportunities to read news from citizen reporters, people on the ground where events are happening. It goes without saying that you can become one too. Any citizen can tweet or share their experience or information about a developing story using one of the social media apps. This is something I have done myself on more than one occasion.

Indeed, major news networks now routinely put out calls on the Internet for information from people who may be living near, or involved in, stories they are covering. A growing number of hybrid news publications allow nearly anyone to write news stories for them, as long as they pass basic tests for skill and accuracy.

Some of these news websites even pay the author royalties on articles and images they contribute. So, if you have always had a hankering to be a journalist or a nose for news, the newsroom of the Internet doesn't just mean being a part of the studio audience. You can become a reporter, too.

The World's Biggest University

It may seem odd at first to describe the Internet as a university. After all, universities conjure up images of lecture halls in which teachers impart decades of wisdom and experience and the content of big, "clunky" textbooks and students take exams to demonstrate they have absorbed all of this.

But make no mistake about this; the Internet *can* be a great university if you let it. As schools and businesses become more comfortable with the Internet, more and more of them are offering courses and even whole degree programs online. For a retiree with a thirsty mind, you need never run out of things to study. The Internet provides many opportunities for intellectual enrichment.

There is the lecture hall of YouTube, a website that continues to be a storehouse of knowledge. On this website, you can search for and then watch actual lectures people have recorded and posted or educational videos made specifically for Internet audiences on every imaginable subject. If there is anything you want to know, type in a "how to _____" phrase into YouTube, and you will usually find informative results much like I did when I used a YouTube video to learn how to do vibrato on a violin, which surprised my teacher.

As with everything on the Internet, in the YouTube lecture hall, you are not obligated to just be a student. Anyone with a webcam or smartphone can upload a personal lecture or "how to" video to the Internet. So with the wealth of knowledge and experience gained over the years, YouTube is a great vehicle that retirees can use to learn from the world, or allow the world to learn from your expertise.

Put the Internet in Your Pocket with a Smartphone

I have mentioned smartphones a number of times in previous chapters. It is now time to examine the benefits of this personal tool. The stereotype of the modern smartphone user is the teenager who is glued to his mobile phone; not looking up at his surroundings or even speaking to those around him. What could he possibly be doing, you may wonder, that is more important than taking in this beautiful day or talking to his family?

The answer is that most teenagers are talking to their friends. We have seen how the Internet makes it easy for persons to "be there" from a distance; but it also makes it tempting to neglect being present in the moment in favor of talking to friends who are outside of our immediate physical space. But like all temptations, those presented by smartphones can be managed in exchange for some potentially great benefits.

Nearly everything we have talked about in this chapter – email, social media, video chatting, information gathering and sharing - can be reached through a smartphone as well as a computer. While it might rightfully seem silly to have a telephone which also allows you to do all these other things, some seniors may find it worth the investment - especially if you plan to travel. Smartphones also double as high-resolution cameras and even video cameras and Global Positioning Systems (GPS) that use satellites to produce a map that shows you exactly where you are at any given time as well as provide directions to anywhere based on your current location. A smartphone can also roughly translate between common languages; be a source of information about any businesses in your immediate area and provide real-time updates about lodging and transportation options.

The combination of smartphone and Internet technology yields several other unique benefits. For example, apps that allow the creation of a group of contacts who can exchange messages and real-time phone calls. I used this once to ensure that a student from Nevis arrived safely in Jamaica even though I was traveling and could not oversee her arrival and settlement in person. I used WhatsApp and created a group consisting of myself, the student, her father and the friend who I had recruited to pick her up from the airport and get her settled in her dorm. In this way, I was able to monitor her movement in real-time throughout the entire process of travel and arrival and be comforted that she got to her destination safely.

For the photographer in all of us, the uses for cameras on smartphones go far beyond the ability to video chat with someone else. A serious photographer probably wants a camera with the desired specifications to take pictures of the highest quality; but a hobbyist who simply wants to capture everyday events and experiences, could be well-served by a smartphone's camera. Gone are the days of tiny, blurry images provided by the earliest camera phones. The built-in camera on today's smartphone rivals the resolution and color balance of yesterday's professional camera. Many of these phones can also take video at the correct resolution to be posted to the Internet. Apps even allow armchair photographers to edit their photos and email or share them to social media, right from their phones.

Of course, sharing your adventures is not the only reason to have a video camera in your pocket. Smartphones can also be used to improve your home's security. An ever-increasing number of merchants are selling relatively inexpensive cameras that can be installed inside or outside the home which can be monitored from your smartphone any time you want. In this way, you can keep an eye on your home or pets while you are away.

I have not specifically mentioned the use of tablets in this discussion although studies show that the tablet is the preferred device for users 35 and over. The tablet can generally do *everything* that a smartphone can, except sending text messages (SMS) and making telephone calls. The tablet has a bigger screen than the smartphone which probably explains its popularity with seniors. For the senior, the bigger screen makes for a better experience reading text, watching videos and video chatting. If your device is a tablet, you can access the same facilities of email, social media, video chatting, photography, internet surfing, information gathering, information sharing and other applications described for smartphones.

E-Commerce

E-commerce is something many people who grew up without the Internet are still reluctant to embrace. Entering your bank account or credit card data into a computer that is connected to the Internet may seem risky; but as e-commerce has exploded over time, websites that send and receive payments have come up with many efficient ways of ensuring the security of your personal information.

Nearly every transaction can be done via the Internet today, if you want to. Bank accounts can be accessed, balances viewed and money transferred online. Most utility services also have online payment systems which may save you money by avoiding late fees and the necessity of using stamps, and paying online definitely saves you time. Some utility companies even give small discounts to people who sign up for auto-pay – automatic electronic withdrawals from their bank accounts each month, which ensure bills get paid on time. Some companies offer special rewards to customers who opt strictly for receiving statements or bills via the Internet and making payments online.

Everyone from big name-brand merchants to local artisans can set up online stores where you simply pay them by putting in your credit or debit card information and they deliver their goods or service right to your door. Clothing, books, airline tickets, art supplies, tools, furniture, groceries – you name it, you can find and purchase it online and have it delivered directly to you as requested.

The biggest savings for the retiree from these methods is in time, transportation costs and sheer hassle. Although some may prefer to see goods themselves before they buy them, or may enjoy getting out of the house from time to time, it is no longer strictly necessary to drive across town and spend an hour shopping if you want something. Now, very often, you can just log in, point and click.

Of course, it goes without saying that if local artisans can use the Internet to sell their goods and services, so can you. Though making money may not be your primary interest in your retirement years, online marketplaces may allow you to get paid for your knowledge and skills, your hobbies, or just for getting rid of old junk. The Internet really does make it easier for you to do whatever you want to do in retirement, including making money off your possessions and skills and the fun things you do.

Stay Safe – Important Dos and Don'ts

While I encourage people to embrace and explore all the Internet has to offer, there are some common sense safety measures which can help to prevent unpleasant experiences.

1. *Physical Safety*

Similar to what happens when meeting people on the street, it is possible to have your personal safety put at risk by someone you met on the Internet. Although the risk is not greater online than in real life, how to prevent this on the Internet may not be as obvious as how to prevent it on the street.

As is the case when you are on the street, the key is to be sensible and alert; do not be caught off guard. Do not give your home address, for example, to someone who you just met and have no reason to trust as yet. You may not even wish to give out your real name until you know persons well enough to be confident that their motives are sincere and you would like to give them access to your real identity. Even when people take the precaution of getting to know someone first, the odd story still arises of a person meeting another online who turned out to be a completely different person in appearance and personality from what was initially portrayed.

So on the Internet, as in real life, use your head.

2. *Monetary and Data Safety*

Far more common than the person who is physically harmed by someone they met on the Internet is the story of someone who was hacked, which may lead to money being drained from one's bank account, false purchases being made under one's name, or even embarrassing information being leaked to the public. Hackers play an ever-evolving game with businesses who want to conduct transactions online; businesses work to keep their customers safe, and hackers work to find a way around these safety systems.

To protect yourself from hacking, I suggest you follow these four basic rules:

1. NEVER give your password to any account to someone via email, even if the email claims to be from, say, your bank. Your bank will never ask you for your password via email.

   Phishing scams that try to convince people they are legitimate sources asking for financial information, personal information or passwords for legitimate reasons are unfortunately quite common. Those of us who are new to the Internet may be especially vulnerable because we generally assume that any email we get is from the person representing to be the sender. But most websites you join will inform you that they will never ask for your password, account details or other personal information via email; so if someone does, do not give them the information. Instead, report them to the website they're impersonating so the web administrator can warn other customers not to fall for the email trick.

2. NEVER access a bank account or put in credit card information when you are using a public wireless (Wi-Fi) network. If you can help it, do not even put in the password for websites that are linked to your bank account or credit card.

    You see, a hacker with the proper skills can see the information being passed back and forth on the Internet by someone on the same network as themselves. So hackers can hang out in, say a coffee shop, or even set up a software program that they attach to the wireless network and just wait to collect the bank or credit card information of customers who decide to login to their bank accounts from the coffee shop.

3. NEVER respond to an email advising that you have won money in a contest, lottery, or sweepstake you have not entered. Unfortunately, these are popular scams intended to entice you to disclose your personal information and con you into releasing funds purportedly for the payment of taxes, insurance and other fees associated with the "winnings."

    Legitimate contests, lotteries and sweepstakes will never ask you to pay any costs at any time in order to cash in on the winnings. Such costs are always deducted from the winnings at source. Any document that is sent to you for completion and signature and that requires you to disclose personal information is likely to be counterfeit, regardless of how official it may appear.

4. CHANGE your passwords frequently and make them good ones.

If your password is hard to figure out and you use different passwords over time, there is less chance that a hacker can steal your password and later use it to impersonate you. The password "6161949" that represents your birthdate may be easy to figure out. On the other hand, the password J#16@49 is much stronger. In this example, I have substituted the capital letter "J" for the 6th month, June, abbreviated the year, and inserted special symbols between the month, day and year. Passwords combining alpha, numeric and special symbols with both capital and common lettering are considered the strongest.

If you find the demand for multiple passwords overwhelming, there are a few ways to help you remember. Some of my tech savvy friends use Google Keychain and similar apps to store all of their website, username, and password information electronically in what they consider a secure method. I must confess I have a hard time with the thought that putting your information all in one place on your computer is a good idea and so I use the good old-fashioned pen-and-paper method.

You can have a piece of paper in a cookbook in the kitchen with a listing of all your account names and passwords. Even if your house was robbed, I doubt the burglar would think of looking in a soufflé cookbook to find anything of value. This important information is certainly secure from online hackers who will look for it on your computer's hard drive.

3. Psychological Safety

By our age, not much shocks us anymore. Yet human nature never fails to turn up surprises, and the Internet is full of them. This generation's biggest Internet surprise is probably the rise of trolling, people who intentionally say horrible things for the sole purpose of upsetting other people.

It is difficult to say what drives these trolls (yes, they are named after the fairy tale monsters that hid under bridges and attacked unsuspecting travelers). Perhaps it is a similar psychology to that of the schoolyard bully. A common Internet adage is "don't feed the trolls," – which means don't give attention to people who are behaving in a very upsetting manner. Don't respond or argue with them. Remember that with trolls, disengaging and ceasing to respond is the ultimate victory for you.

BestPlaceForSeniors.com – A home for the Young at Heart

Now that I have taken you through the many benefits - and possible risks - of the Internet, I want to close with a reminder of the Internet's purpose for retirees and introduce you to the website I created, http://www. BestPlaceForSeniors.com.

There are no *shoulds* in retirement. If you choose to take advantage of some of the benefits of the Internet outlined here, great; but keep safety in mind so that you can have an enjoyable experience. To take that experience to the ultimate level, engage the help of younger, tech-savvy members of your family who I am sure will be happy to show off their own skills. They can take you through the rudiments of the technology and lend considerable assistance to your efforts to create and experiment. If you choose to remain a non-digital creature, that is great too. Just remember that the Internet's tools are there, if you should ever need them.

The website, BestPlaceForSeniors.com, promotes the basic thesis of this book; that retirement is a time to engage in an active, fun-filled lifestyle and there are many activities through which this engagement can be undertaken. It promotes the use of technology among seniors and dispels the myth that the Internet is a "bad" place. The website encourages seniors across cultures and borders to get connected and provides a forum for sharing thoughts and learning about other cultures and customs. It provides an opportunity for seniors to teach each other "new tricks." I would encourage everyone who reads this book to join the community of seniors at BestPlaceForSeniors.com and add to the richness of our collective online experience.

Tell Your Story

As retirees, we have full, rich, life stories to tell. Our own lives are chapters in the history of the world. Our memoirs could doubtless fill books, and the knowledge, experiences, and identities we pass on could be invaluable to younger generations.

Now that you have a chance to step back and reflect on your life in a more relaxed frame of mind, there are many reasons for you to consider telling your story. One is philanthropic: you have seen and learned a lot, and both your own children and grandchildren, and the world at large, may benefit from having your memories preserved in detail. But the other is a deeply personal reason and is perhaps even more compelling: the act of telling your story will give *you* valuable new insights into your life, your struggles and triumphs, and where you fit both in the intimate history of your own family tree and in the broader picture of human history.

Past generations were more limited in their ability to preserve their memories for us. Even as recently as our parents' generation, many of our parents never learned to type; likely did not have video or audio recording technology available to them; and even if they were technically able to record their stories, this was such a new and seemingly self-centered idea that probably very few of them would even have thought of doing such a thing.

We all know what this results in; historians who struggle to recover pieces of the past from those old books and images that do survive, debating endlessly about how people really felt and experienced the world in past eras, and facing uncertainties about what really happened in the past that will probably never be solved. On a more personal level, it results in persons like myself having absolutely no knowledge of the personalities and lives of any of my grandparents who all passed on before I was born.

Some of us may take it for granted that we do not know where we came from. But how would we view our own triumphs and tragedies if we knew whose grandchildren we were, or what our parents experienced at our age? Would we view the ongoing march of history differently if we had a first-hand account of what came before? In this era of technology, rapid cultural change, and recognition of the importance of every person's identity and experience, the time has never been better for us retirees to tell our stories. For it is in telling our stories and hearing those of our forebears, that we begin to learn who we truly are.

Going Back to Your Roots

Each of our stories is part of the vast and sweeping patchwork of history. There may be many things we do not know, even about our own parents, that might yield surprising insights about who we are. Your story may be more colorful than you ever imagined; your parents and grandparents may be activists, rebels, adventurers, brave soldiers and generally involved in history in ways that you have never thought about.

They may even have registered significant firsts in some important aspects of national or community life, achievements that you certainly would want to know about and celebrate in retrospect.

A growing number of services exist today which compile historical records from hundreds of sources and attempt to use these to allow people to learn about their own family trees. As technology advances, some services are even beginning to offer affordable DNA tests, which will tell you exactly which genetic markers you have in your own cells. These genetic markers arose in different populations over time across the globe, so they can tell you what percentage of your DNA comes from different ethnic groups, where and when you shared ancestors with other ethnic groups, and more.

While these broad, sweeping vistas of history are certainly enlightening and make us realize how much we have in common with others, the immediate past is of more interest to us on a personal level. What careers did our grandparents have? Where did our parents live and grow up? What was it like to live in these past eras which directly gave rise to the culture and attitudes of today?

One relative of mine, Elmer, chose to discover this in a very intimate and immediate way by taking a trip back to his grandparents' homestead. I interviewed him for this book, asking him to share his experience of traveling back to this place which was of such importance to understanding his own personal history. When Elmer realized his grandchildren were growing up with little idea or experience of their ancestral roots, he decided to change that dynamic. So, in the summer of 2015, he arranged a family vacation to visit his grandparents' homestead in Texas where he had spent many of his formative years over half a century ago.

The house had stood empty since 1962 when the winds of change shifted and scattered branches of the family tree far and wide, leaving only the proud old building steeped in decades of history and the memories of those who had lived within its walls. While many people may not be able to go back to their childhood home and find it exactly as it was when they left, Elmer had this unique opportunity, and the experience made a real impression in giving him and his family historical perspective.

Perhaps a similar impression might be made on you and yours by describing your family home and daily routine in great detail either in writing, audio, or video formats. Often it is the small ways in which day-to-day life changes across the decades, the things we take for granted and do not notice, which really add up to big cultural "aha!" moments. It already boggles the minds of Elmer's grandchildren to think that he had no cell phone growing up, and that many foods they can now buy at any supermarket were luxuries to him and his siblings. How much might those differences have changed Elmer's experience of everyday life and the way he thinks about the world?

When Elmer returned to his grandparents' home he noticed both the benefits and costs of leaving a building untouched for half a century. Without maintenance or protection from the ravages of time, a small part of the roof had fallen in. And yet, so many memories and pieces of history still remained in patches of living color. Dishes and food were still in the cabinets. His grandmother's purse, dating from when she was a young and fashionable woman, was still in the closet. So was his grandfather's sport coat which was worn to so many social events in an era so different from our own.

Elmer was even able to find one of his old classmates still living in town. The thought of their grandfather in high school must be quite a trip for his teenage grandsons. For me, I cannot think of many experiences that are more surreal than seeing my own grandmother and grandfather as handsome and stylish twenty-somethings in old photos, preparing to embark on life's great adventures with no knowledge of where these events would take them. With nothing preserved, I have little sense of who my grandparents were. At times, I wonder how it would have affected my own perception of life over the years to have known the details of my ancestors' lives, the things they lived through and experienced at my age.

Elmer found the experience of physically returning to his own roots with the younger generations of his family very rewarding. He was proud to be able to share so much of their heritage with them in a time when so many young people grow up with little knowledge on what the world used to be like, how life has changed, and what changes are still to come in the decades ahead.

Seeing their grandfather's childhood home in vivid detail; complete with food in the pantry, furniture of the house still in place, their great-great grandmother's purse still in the closet and their great-great grandfather's sport jacket still hanging on the rod, surely helped give these teenagers a sense of their roots. So much of who we are now can be explained by our lineage.

While a vacation back to your childhood home may not be feasible or desirable for everyone, for those who can, visiting ancestral homes and landmarks is an unparalleled way to give younger generations of your family a sense of history, and to recapture that sense for yourself. Such a visit could help tremendously when you tell your story for future generations. With the facilities for photography, film, and audio recording more accessible than ever before, you can capture your past while walking through the rooms where you slept as a child, or through the hallways of the schools you attended

Even if you prefer the medium of writing to film or video, remember that taking a physical trip back in time could greatly inspire you with the details and feelings of the places of your youth. There is no better way to preserve the past than to go there, and take your audience with you.

Your Place in History

Mention of "your place in history" may make you feel old. Because, after all, schools teach historical events that happened hundreds of years ago which makes us think of history as being something that is over, or which is very, very old. But that view is a misconception. History is nothing more or less than the happenings of the present, seen in retrospect. History is happening around us and we are helping to create it all the time. Everyone alive today is a part of history; although some of us have more personal history accumulated than others.

Where were you when the first human set foot on the Moon? When the Space Shuttle Challenger exploded, taking with it seven NASA crew including the woman who was expected to be the first teacher in space? When the World Trade Center attacks of 9/11/2001 ushered in a new era of global terrorism? What cultural and technological changes have you lived through? What triumphs and tribulations?

No matter what your personal story is, I can guarantee that it speaks to history; whether you were supported or suffered under the social attitudes of a bygone era, embraced an identity or self-image characteristic of your times, found success or challenges in a changing job market, or even faced a true triumph or tragedy such as war or the effects of a world-changing discovery; these are things people will be writing about in history books someday. Take this opportunity to put in your "two cents" now.

For your family, what life lessons can you pass to them? What do you wish someone had told you, or wish that you had done differently, fifty years ago? Ten years ago? Last week? (Remember, I said history is happening all the time.) What are your concerns and cautions for the young people around you, considering how the world they are growing into has changed, and will continue to change? What do you hope they will do to develop themselves, and the world?

Lastly, and perhaps most importantly, there is the personal aspect. What triumphs and tragedies formed you in childhood and beyond? What obstacles did you face because of your family's history or the broader circumstances of the time? What critical health challenges have you battled and overcome? How did it feel when things went well with history, or when they went badly? How have the identities passed down to you from family, and those you have painstakingly carved for yourself created the story of the *you* that others see today?

How do all of these changes, triumphs and tragedies form the story of you? I am so inspired by my dear friend, Dr. Jennifer Mamby-Alexander who tells her own story of cancer survival in the book *A Practical Guide to Coping with Cancer*. This book chronicles what she learned in staring down this very frightening illness which, in Jennifer's words, "felt like being in shark-infested waters waiting for them to pick us off one by one." Her story of how she coped with the knowledge that she had cancer with an uncertain survival rate has provided countless others with hope, wisdom and a sense that they are not alone in their struggle.

Jennifer has even been able to bring about change for cancer survivors by using her own medical expertise to open the Hair Loss Clinic of Jamaica to help cancer survivors feel normal and return to normal lives. This just goes to show that history is not made by great people in some faraway land; it is made by people just like you and me. This is why we should share our stories; who knows what history we have made that we are taking for granted?

Choose Your Medium: To Write, Snap, or Record?

The modern era puts both writing and recording technology within reach of practically everyone. This leads to some interesting considerations about the costs and benefits of each. For me, nothing is better for really getting inside someone else's experience than reading and writing. In books, we can see not just what something looks like, but also exactly what someone is thinking. There are nuances to how we see the world that can be communicated in words that simply cannot be communicated on camera. Reading any good book and then comparing it to the movie will show you that.

Books also have the advantage of being fairly immune to changes in technology. While in this modern era DVDs may someday become obsolete just like VHS tapes before them, anyone who can read will always be able to read a book on paper. Imagine accumulating a library of family memoirs; your grandchildren and great-grandchildren could read your life story, and those of your children and their children as they grew up. Imagine what it is like to be a child with this opportunity; you are reading a great biography like one you might encounter in history class, but you know this is the story of your very own grandparent.

However, there are also some unique benefits to film. It is certainly a very visual medium which can make things come alive for modern audiences. If persons are sitting there looking at you, you know these are not fictional characters you are reading about. If they are in a room that is decorated like a room out of the past, or if they are showing you objects from their own history, you get a sense of such rooms, and such objects, more than you would from a book. Shape, color, texture, and size are all right there.

Where an author might shrink from describing every detail of a room in a book for good reason, video can give a sense of detail and what it was really like to live in a place or time more thoroughly than a book can. So what is your fancy? Would you rather communicate your innermost thoughts and feelings and your past and present insights about the world in the form of a book? Or would you rather give your viewers a sense of the immediacy and reality of the past using a visual medium?

Say it with Pictures – Film and Photographs

There is a saying that a picture is worth a thousand words. Having seen pictures of my friends' parents and grandparents, I can say that really is true. Photographs are a very visual way of recording memories that really capture the atmosphere and feeling of a time and place. I envy friends of mine who have photographs of their parents, grandparents, or even great-grandparents as children and young adults. Having a visual history of their family really helps to ground them in a sense of time. They can see their grandparents as children, wearing Edwardian garb like we see in historical romances; and their parents as young adults, looking like characters out of *Casablanca*.

Whether from recent years or generations past, your family probably has a wealth of photographic history. You may even be able to add to it using resources like Ancestry.com, which may have public records, including photographs of relatives that you do not have in your possession. Either way, one thing is for sure; in this age of polaroids and instagrams you will have plenty of photographic material to draw on from recent decades.

The challenge, then, is what do you want your photographic story to say? Do you want it to have a humorous feel or a dramatic one? Do you want it to be far-reaching, spanning deep into history; or do you want to focus on yourself and on your children, creating an intimate and personal family photo journal?

As with all things in this century, photo books can be created both in the old-fashioned way of physically putting together a scrapbook and digitally using various scanning and software applications. Some companies will even allow you to upload photographs and then arrange them into various configurations within a book. These services will then print copies of the book for you, complete with a hardback binding. Photo editing software programs also exist to allow you to change the color of photos or combine several different photos together. One service offered by some professional photo editors, for example, is that of memorial portraits – where the editor will photoshop a deceased loved one into photos to represent them being present in spirit.

When curating photographs, as when curating stories, start by gathering up photos and seeing what you have. Perhaps some photographs will jump out at you and demand to be turned into something. These treasured visual memories can become books and full family histories, or they can become gifts, commemorating important life events.

Photographs can also be combined with other technology such as audio recording and even video, into digital slide shows. You could have a tech-savvy younger relative help you record yourself telling the stories of the photographs you have curated, and then overlay your voice narration on a digital slideshow. You could even include video clips if these were also available and formed part of the story you wish to tell.

Of course, the ultimate medium which combines images with words is video. Imagine having your own parents or grandparents on video, telling you the story of their lives. Perhaps they will have major events to share, such as their experience growing up in an area affected by war or another event of global significance. Perhaps they lived through, or were part of, some major cultural revolution or Renaissance. Perhaps they saw huge economic catastrophes and shifts that have created the world we see today. Perhaps they were witness to the harrowing effects of natural disasters? Or perhaps they are just people like you, who can tell you what they wish they had known at your age.

Even if you are not a filmmaker yourself, do not despair. If you really want to go high tech, the wider availability of technology means that there are many freelance filmmakers in your town or a nearby city who can be hired for reasonable prices. If you are feeling more like a do-it-yourselfer, your young relatives probably have sufficient technical skills to assist you with the project. Just tell them what you want and watch how skillfully they manipulate webcams, camera phones and video editing software to produce it. And what better way to really bring your story home for them than to have them helping you to record and produce it?

Whether you want to tell your story in a book or on video, there will be writing to do. In a book that may be obvious; but in a video, it is equally important to plan the questions you want to ask and how you want to answer them; how you want to frame your story so that the viewer has a coherent, thought-provoking experience; and just generally how to turn the messy, unpredictable business of life into a condensed package that is really valuable for both you and others.

Writing, for Books or Film: How to Tell a Story

The first misconception I want to address is that a book or video has to be some great, long work of literature. It doesn't. In fact, in literature, shorter is sometimes better. Each year, for example, Houghton Mifflin Harcourt Publishing releases a volume of *The Best American Essays*. These are pieces of profound writing, between ten and thirty pages, that usually draw heavily from the writers' own life experiences.

Before you form a fixed image in your head of what you want to write or shoot on video, consider the different forms available. Do you want to write an autobiography? One or more essays sharing your thoughts and experiences? If you have a literary or dramatic flair, are you interested in writing short stories or performance pieces about your life? Do you like poetry?

I myself have found a light-hearted way of honoring the past – by turning my experiences into short, comical stories that I tell as performance pieces. These humorous recollections of shared history evoke howls of laughter at family and community events as audience members see parts of themselves in the personal experiences I share.

If you are interested in sharing your story with more than just your family, there are many ways to reach the wider world. Perhaps the most obvious is by submitting your story, essay, or book for traditional publication. Among other things, the Internet makes it easier than ever before to connect with publications, publishing houses, and even enter competitions that may be looking for creative works. The Internet also makes it easier than ever before to self-publish a book; that is, to order a printing of paper copies, or turn your book into a digital e-book that anyone can purchase on Amazon.com and read on their computer, phone, or e-reader.

Once you have given some thought to what types of storytelling you would like to do – video or writing, in a long-form book or in shorter pieces for public or private consumption, – it is time to start thinking about how to structure your story.

Make an Outline

If you have a long story to tell, it is a good idea when brainstorming to make an outline of the most important events that you want to be sure you cover. Depending on how ambitious you are feeling, you can make this outline any length; from just a few points whose reality and relationship to each other you really want to explore in depth, to many points that you want to weave into an overarching life story. Very likely, you will go through a few versions of these outlines, adding or removing events as you work and realize that something is too much, or is missing.

Once you have a rough list of events that feel important for you to think and write about, start thinking and writing about them. As with song writing, it is best to have some really rough material and raw thoughts to help illuminate what is going on in your head. It can even be helpful to have an audio recorder handy; especially if you have thoughts come to you when you are on the go. You are much more likely to make a record of these if you can just speak them and capture them on your audio recorder or smartphone, than if you have to stop what you are doing, turn on a computer or find a pad of paper to write them down. The smartphone also offers you a useful "memo" facility to make notes.

What are the first things that come out when you sit down to write a page about your childhood? About your teenage years? About life in your twenties? As you are reading back over your own "brain vomit" (as a friend of mine is fond of calling this first exercise of writing whatever comes to mind), do you see anything that strikes you as warranting more exploration or development? It is when we sit down to face a blank piece of paper with a question like one of these on our mind that we truly see and re-experience a particular event or time of life.

One trap to be careful of when processing your life story is your own preconceptions. You might have ideas about how you *want* to believe the story went, or what is or is not good to talk about. There might be things you are afraid to say or admit to, things you would rather sweep under the rug, or things you consider so unimportant that you think it is boring to the reader to mention them.

Ultimately, you have both the right and responsibility to choose what goes into the life story you share with the world. But the tale which is most valuable both to yourself and others will be the truest one, not a manicured version of how you think you should present yourself to others. There is real value in the messiness of life - so I would urge you to write as honestly as possible in your brainstorm and to carefully examine anything that comes out that makes you feel uncomfortable.

How many times have you found yourself recounting some story or fact from your youth that seemed logical to you, but which fascinated or shocked the younger people in the room? How many times have you seen younger people going about their daily lives and thought to yourself, "I'll bet they can't imagine what it was like when _____"?

You may think young folks are not interested in hearing from you; and maybe as teenagers, they are not. But I was not fortunate enough to have my own father or mother tell me their stories before they passed away. Now, in my adulthood, there are so many questions I wish I could have asked them. You can do your children and grandchildren a favor by answering these questions for them now as you tell your story.

Ask Questions

Once you have brainstormed and written an outline, it is time to dive deeper. For each event on your brainstorming list try answering the following questions to elucidate more interesting insights:

1. How do you remember feeling during this event? Are there triggers related to this event that involve sights, sounds and smells? What thoughts did you have while it was going on? (This is an equally valid question no matter how old you were at the time, be it three years or thirty.)
2. How did the people around you react to this event? Friends, family members, neighbors, employers, fellow employees?
3. How did this event change your life? Even if it is something as routine or minor as starting at a new school or having an argument with someone, how did it change your daily life from then on? Did someone's attitude change as a result of the argument?
4. What was going on nationally or globally at the time this event was happening to you? This can lend some really interesting historical

perspective. Even if you are talking about something local like when you met your life partner, you can provide the reader or viewer with interesting historical contexts that happened at the same time. Let them know if the meeting happened on the same day the first person walked on the Moon, or around the time a given national leader was elected to office.

5. Looking back from your current viewpoint, what would you have told your past self about that situation? Would you have consoled, rejoiced, or recommended a different course of action?

6. Did you have thoughts about the future at this point in your life? What did you think your future was to be like? The future of the world?

7. What choices did you make and what actions did you take, consciously or unconsciously, that affected the outcome of this situation? Were you the instigator of change or the determiner of what occurred, or were you an unwilling, unwitting participant? If you choose to write about things outside the scope of your own immediate experience, such as the experiences of your parents, grandparents, or even older ancestors - these questions can still be useful. In the process of asking those questions you may even end up remembering things they told you, or if these honored relatives are still around, you could interview them too.

Interviewing people who were involved in your life story is an important and instructive part of the process. Nobody has his or her life story happen all alone; and interviewing those around you about the events you shared is an invaluable opportunity to reconnect, encourage others to share their own stories, and even learn new things you never knew before about the people and events that are part of your life.

Pruning and Cultivating

Depending on how ambitious you were starting out, and how ambitious you are now, after a few steps into the endeavor of exploring your life story you may find you have more content than you can handle. If you plan to only make an hour-long video, are looking at a 100-page book, or simply feel that what you have so far is messy and overwhelming, it might be time to look at what you have created as a whole using your outline and the questions above.

At this point, your intuition is probably all the guide you need. If something seems repetitive or predictable, look for ways to mix it up with rephrasing and reframing. If you really feel like it does not need to be there, cut it out.

As you look back over your notes and the draft so far, are you seeing common themes emerge, such as external influences that have affected many of your life events, or common trends in your own behaviors and choices? These themes may be worth considering when creating an overall narrative, and eventually, a title for your life story. One example that comes to mind is the title of Leah Remini's autobiography which she named after a personality trait for which she was criticized throughout her life, but which has ultimately allowed her to make positive change in the world. She called her memoir *Troublemaker*.

Now, I hope you are well on your way to telling your life story. This therapeutic and beneficial exercise is a great way to leave your legacy for the future and may turn out to be the most fun-filled activity you pursue in retirement.

Conclusion

Retirement is an end of sorts: an end to the rigid, structured life imposed by the workplace. It is an end to responsibilities and stresses not of our own choosing – and the beginning of a life we do choose.

We come into retirement from a background that is planned for us. For that reason, we can understand the image of retirement as a mere loss of work. With no one to tell us what to do with our days some may ask, "What do I do now?" Another stark reality at this stage of our lives is the fact that our children and those we have cared for have all grown up, moved out and moved on with their lives, independent of us. With empty nests and time on our hands, we again face the dilemma of what to do now.

I have attempted to offer some answers in this book.

Retirement is the time to realize the things we have wanted to do over the years. We are never "too old" to travel, learn a musical instrument, or pick up another hobby. Free from the nine-to-five grind, this is our time to explore what gives us personal joy. Studies show that for most people, happiness comes not from comfort and convenience, but from facing and surmounting challenges. Joy also comes from helping others – and in this respect, we retirees have so much to offer. There is no substitute for experience, and through mentorship and volunteerism we can share our experience with others.

The Information Age offers us new ways to realize our dreams that were not available to generations past. The Internet makes it easier than ever before to connect with like-minded people, learn new skills, and share things we have created.

I hope that the resources shared here will assist readers in following their dreams. There are so many resources available to us today that allow us to learn; to become artists; to volunteer; and to travel without breaking the bank. It is my hope that you explore them all.

My mother taught me to use my time on this earth wisely; to not waste any time fitting stereotypes or doubting my own abilities. Retirement was not an end for her, but rather, a long-awaited beginning. I watched her live that potential to its fullest, and she inspired me to do the same.

I feel lucky now, in my own retirement, to be able to bring this same message to you. Whether you are long-retired or pre-retired or if you are waiting for a sign to pursue your dreams, this book is that sign. Consider me the friendly push that tells you, "Now is your time. Go for it!" The most fulfilling life is not the more convenient and comfortable life – rather, it is the life in which adventures are had, challenges are faced, and triumphs are won. This is true whether you are retired or pre-retired. It is never too late or too early to begin living the adventures of which you have always dreamed.

What will *your* adventures be?

"There is evidence in this book, that Patricia Reid-Waugh has spent much time in contemplation and reflection, perhaps leading up to, and certainly during, retirement. Despite a life steeped in quantitative pursuits – Mathematics, Accounting and Finance – her mastery of language allows for a remarkably rhythmic flow of words. She is able to successfully take the reader on an exploration of the wide variety of possibilities which can be considered in order to plan for and pursue fun-filled, active and rewarding experiences in retirement. Whether the reader is young and pre-retired or mature and retired, as Reid-Waugh weaves anecdotes from her rich personal experiences and those of others and shares tips and advice reflecting her mastery of traditional methods and contemporary technology, savoring the tapestry she produced in this book and sharing it with others is inevitable."

Lilieth H. Nelson, PhD

About the Author

Patricia Reid-Waugh spent her early working life as a teacher of mathematics before returning to university to complete a master's degree in accounting. She then pursued an extensive professional accountancy career with Deloitte firms in Jamaica and St. Maarten and later served as Regulator of the Financial Services for the island of Nevis. She retired from the working world in 2011.

Patricia's multicultural exposure is complimented by her broad creative and social pursuits, a great sense of humor, and a passion for life. She plays the piano and organ and writes poetry and short stories for entertainment at community and family events.

Since retirement, Patricia has taken up the challenge of learning to play the violin, determined to dispel the myth that "you can't teach an old dog new tricks." Now she has ventured into the world of literary publication with this, her first book.

Printed in the United States
By Bookmasters